Let There Be Peace in the Classroom

Jenni Douglas Duncan

DISCIPLESHIP RESOURCES

PO BOX 340003 • NASHVILLE, TN 37203-0003
www.discipleshipresources.org

Cover and book design by Nanci H. Lamar
Edited by Debra D. Smith and Heidi L. Hewitt

Photograph of author on back cover © Olan Mills. Used by permission.

ISBN 0-88177-385-9
Library of Congress Control Number 2002103374

DR385

Contents

Chapter One

Introduction

Our God Is a God of Peace

Columbine. West Bank. World Trade Center. These are not just names of places anymore; they evoke unforgettable images and memories of violence. A fear within us asks, *Is there hope for peace?* Our faith says yes.

In Romans 15:33 and in many other passages, Paul refers to God as the "God of peace." Just as *almighty* describes God, so does *peace*. Christians understand the melodic words of Isaiah 9:6 to refer to Jesus: "For a child has been born for us,...and he is named Wonderful Counselor, Mighty God, Everlasting Father, Prince of Peace."

Scripture shows that peace is not God's sideline, something God moonlights at when the real work is done. *Shalom*, the Hebrew word for peace, means much more than a lack of conflict. It means wholeness, being right with God and neighbors. It is a close relative of the word *salvation*. In contrast, a lack of peace means brokenness, sin, estrangement, and a need for God's healing and forgiveness.

Peace is central to God, so we need to treat it seriously. However, we have not always done so. Children must surely wonder, *If our Creator is a God of peace, why is the world so violent?* The child of the information age knows of war and violence in faraway lands and worries about it erupting at school.

In a child's world, peace is broken with more than guns and knives. Belittling and name-calling can destroy a child's hope for personal peace. When a child is excluded at recess, picked on at school, belittled or treated unfairly after school, he or she feels helpless when no one intervenes.

When people feel hopeless and helpless, they often fill the void with violence, vengeance, or despair. Children who are left out, excluded, or bullied need shalom. They need peace within and peacemaking skills. So, of course, do those who mistreat them.

The good news is that we can give children peace skills, tools to bring them help and hope. We adults can open the toolbox and show children how to listen, how to solve problems, and how to pray for and practice peace.

What Can a Teacher Do?

The most important thing a teacher can do is to cultivate peace of mind and spirit in his or her own life. Children are looking for role models and watching what adults do. You can bring peace with you into the classroom by your own personal spiritual practices. You can also model peace skills and show children how to form a caring community.

Another avenue of peace building is conflict resolution. In Sunday school or afterschool care, you can teach children to recognize and work through conflict. In Mother's Day Out or Kids' Club, you can give children language to talk about emotions and problems. Any teacher can help children develop skills, such as the following, that enable them to cope with disagreements and problems:

- Developing vocabulary for feelings and learning to identify feelings
- Brainstorming possible endings and solutions to common incidents in the classroom or group
- Listening skills

What do these skills have to do with peace? Obviously, it is hard to solve conflicts if you do not listen well. Feelings also have much to do with any conflict resolution. Children have to learn words for feelings and associate body language with the words.

Simple things such as playing charades can help. A child can demonstrate frustration, for example, by pantomiming attempting to thread a bead on a string, pouting when he or she cannot do it, and then stomping. Children begin to recognize frustration when it occurs.

Even toddlers and preschoolers can develop empathy for others' feelings: Jeremy is about to burst into tears. Ryan walks up and offers Jeremy a car. Jeremy looks happier. You teach vocabulary: "Look, Jeremy was sad that his mother left, but now he feels calmer because he has a friend."

Stories also teach about feelings and behavior. Neither preschool children nor elementary children analyze their own behavior easily. However, they can comment on how a character or puppet behaves or feels.

Classroom Discipline

Broken peace is more than a global or personal issue, for it affects the interactions in your classroom. As a teacher, you may experience less-than-perfect peace in the classroom. Some children are impulsive; some do not cooperate; some are physically aggressive. You may wonder if there is such a thing as a peaceful classroom.

"Peace be with you" was the first thing Jesus said when he appeared to the assembled disciples after his resurrection (Luke 24:36). Peace is a fruit of the Spirit, a promise we can claim for ourselves and for the children we teach. Let there be peace in the classroom.

Chapter Two

Let Peace Begin With Me

The everyday things you do are important. When conflict erupts, you can patiently model negotiation and compromise. When the class has a problem and you suggest a solution that everyone can live with, you demonstrate that no one will be the loser in the class. You teach peace-making as you live out your faith and your commitment to peace.

A teacher can also create an oasis, a refuge from everything that bombards us. This varies from planning for a calm nursery to setting up peace-and-quiet reflection moments for school-agers. Peace begins with you, the teacher. An old adage says, "You can give away only what you have." To give children peace tools, you need to develop your own sense of peace with God and with yourself.

Fill the Reservoir Within You

Imagine trying to serve water or punch from a drink dispenser, but nothing comes from the spigot. You look inside and discover that the liquid is too low to even reach the spigot. That happens to us sometimes in our spiritual life. In the language of 2 Corinthians 4:7, we are clay jars—fragile and broken, yes, but also containers. We need to let God's Spirit fill us so that we have some of Jesus' living water to share. To teach peace, you need to become a reservoir of peace. You can fill your reservoir in various ways: with sabbath, with silence, with prayer, with serenity, and with play.

Keeping a Sabbath Rhythm

Why do we have a sabbath? A sabbath is for rest, of course, and we observe it in obedience to God's instructions. A sabbath is also a time to set aside our perspective and get God's vision for our lives.

When I commuted forty-five miles through the Ouachita Mountains, the beauty made the Creator's majesty manifest. It put my problems and puzzles in perspective. The journey home was also a time to release the day and really be home when I pulled into the driveway. The uninterrupted quiet helped drain away the stress of the day. The weekly rhythm of time at work and time at home brought peace. My week had a sabbath rhythm. When I moved closer to work and could access work through e-mail and networks, it became harder to find that time when I was truly at rest. I miss my mountain time. It makes me think of something the Bible says:

> Get you up to a high mountain, O Zion, herald of good tidings; lift up your voice with strength, O Jerusalem, herald of good tidings, lift it up, do not fear; say to the cities of Judah, "Here is your God!"... To whom then will you compare me, or who is my equal? says the Holy One. Lift up your eyes on high and see: Who created these? He who brings out their host and numbers them, calling them all by name; because he is great in strength, mighty in power, not one is missing.... Have you not known? Have you not heard? The LORD is the everlasting God, the Creator of the ends of the earth. He does not faint or grow weary; his understanding is unsearchable. He gives power to the faint, and strengthens the powerless.   (Isaiah 40:9, 25-26, 28-29)

We need the perspective of the mountaintop. It tells us that God is our creator and that God cares for us.

We cannot fully grasp peace when we ignore how God has created our bodies. The human system has a biorhythm and natural sleep patterns. Genesis 1 tells us that we need a rhythm for work and rest, a sabbath to our lives. We all need a balance of time apart and time together, of time producing or time doing, and of time being. In fact, our relationships with others and our productivity are improved when we take the rest and time apart that we need.

Attending worship on Sunday may not be a true sabbath if the remainder of the day someone or something is always claiming our attention. Our peace can be stolen by our penchant for instant availability. We always have e-mail and voice mail to check, phones to answer, or supplies to buy (even late at night). A sense of peace may require us making choices as to what we will and will not do. Peace may mean giving work and worries to God and focusing on the present moment. That requires discipline, but it brings peace. If you wonder, *Did Eva call about the field trip?*, breathe a prayer, "Jesus, I give it to you." My mom says, "The whole world is not on our shoulders." What peace it is to know that God is in control.

Peace Like Still Waters

In our noisy world, the radio plays in the car and in the store. Television shows are background noise in many homes. When printers and video games are quiet, computers and refrigerators are still humming. If we allow God the silent times, we might hear his whispers better. Elijah found God in the silence.

> He said, "Go out and stand on the mountain before the LORD, for the LORD is about to pass by." Now there was a great wind,...but the LORD was not in the wind; and after the wind an earthquake, but the LORD was not in the earthquake; and after the earthquake a fire, but the LORD was not in the fire; and after the fire a sound of sheer silence. When Elijah heard it, he wrapped his face in his mantle and went out and stood at the entrance of the cave. Then there came a voice to him. (1 Kings 19:11-13)

Today, how could we ever hear the sound of sheer silence? Do you know where you could steep in silence, letting peace sink into your soul? You might seek silence by walking a labyrinth (a prayer pilgrimage; see "About the Labyrinth," on page 119) at a retreat center, in a small park, or in your own backyard. A friend of mine enjoys a quiet devotion while waiting in the carpool line to pick up her child. A retreat is more an attitude than a place. An empty sanctuary can suddenly overflow with God's presence. Try balancing sound with silence to increase your sense of peace.

Silence does not have to mean isolation. At a retreat session, two hundred people sat in auditorium chairs, looking at pictures and reflecting. Silence settled like a vast blanket over everyone there. I was one of them, and I felt God's presence in the silence.

Prayer in a Caring Community

Sabbath, silence, and time alone do not complete the recipe for peace. We also need the grace we find as we practice Christian disciplines with others. We find great solace and support when we pray week after week in a small group or with prayer partners. I feel a lump in my throat every time someone prays for me by name. I am once again surprised at the unearned closeness of God's love, expressed through human voice. I feel a release inside, a realization that God answers and touches my life through people around me. I find hope.

Furthermore, when we feel responsible to pray for the concerns of others, grace flourishes in our own lives. Praying for others touches our own hearts. Sometimes I remind others, and sometimes they remind me, to give it to Jesus.

> Therefore do not worry, saying, "What will we eat?" or "What will we drink?" or "What will we wear?" For it is the Gentiles who strive for all these things; and indeed your heavenly Father knows that you need all these things. But strive first for the kingdom of God and his righteousness, and all these things will be given to you as well. (Matthew 6:31-33)

Choose Patience or Prodding

Sometimes peace begins with some evaluation, making a conscious choice whether to be patient or to seek a solution to a problem. After all, some problems just need our patience. Our children may have to learn some lessons for themselves. Disease or compulsive behavior in others is beyond our control, so we have to let go of our feelings of responsibility.

On the other hand, some problems must be addressed. If we are hurt or angry at family members, it often shows up in bitterness, distance, or passive-aggressive behavior. Sometimes we will not have inner peace unless we work out interpersonal problems with our loved ones. This is not venting but doing the hard work to resolve differences.

Conflict-resolution techniques such as the following work well: cool down before talking, take turns listening as the other person speaks, suggest multiple resolutions, consider the pros and cons, and choose one resolution together with the understanding that you will work through things again if it does not work.

The Serenity Prayer sums it up: "God, grant me the serenity to accept the things I cannot change, courage to change the things I can, and wisdom to know the difference."

Play Is Re-creation

Perhaps for you play is wrestling in autumn leaves with your three-year-old or completing word puzzles with your mother. Maybe you like playing board games on family night, tossing balls, or floating in the pool. We all need play that is not for competition, play that lets us laugh, imagine, and just enjoy the moment. We tend to forget that recreation is for re-creation: renewal, reintegrating who we are, rediscovering the Creator's touch in us. These things happen through play.

We also learn a lot about one another when we play together. Some theorists call play children's brain food, but adults also learn when they play. Play is most important because none of us is whole without it.

Sabbath. Silence. Prayer. Serenity. Play. Make these part of your routine, and you will find that you approach your class in a more peaceful frame of mind.

Try It Out

It is easier to describe what you do than to teach something you do not do. Try out some ways to find your personal mountaintop or to fill your reservoir of peace. Examine your schedule each week for time in which you could seek silence, pray, or take a few hours or a day for a personal retreat. Use any of the exercises below.

Exercise 1

Look for connections between the Scriptures below. Also mark words that jump out at you. As you read about these concepts, make notes about what you could say about fairness or unfairness, justice or injustice. What about wholeness or balance? What about peace itself?

1 Samuel 8:3	Zechariah 7:9
2 Chronicles 19:4-9	Matthew 11:28-30
Psalm 7:8-11; 33; 89:14; 97; 101	Luke 18:1-8; 20:46-47
Isaiah 59:14-16 or 32:15-17; 40	1 Corinthians 14:33
Hosea 2:18-19; 12:6	2 Corinthians 13:11
Amos 5:21-24	Philippians 4:9
Micah 3:5-12	2 Peter 1:1-7

Exercise 2

Do a peace word study using a concordance to find Scripture references about peace. Ask yourself these questions about the Scriptures you read:
• What does this Scripture say about peace?
• Does the Scripture provide any insight about how I might experience the peace of God in my own life?

Exercise 3

Competing commitments create a battle for time for many people. The biblical idea of temperance suggests that finding balance requires moderation in most things. Balance should not be our final goal, though.

God wants wholeness for us:
- An integration of all that we are
- Recognition of where we belong and who we are
- Wellness and salvation

As you reflect on these questions about what your life is like, listen for God's response. Then write your answers in a journal.
- What choices make my life a tangle or a burden?
- Where have I overreached my limits?
- Who am I?
- What has God made unique about me?
- What is my call?
- What purpose do I have?
- For what has God given me my gifts?
- What do I long for?
- What dream is inside me?
- In what ways do I need to wait for God's time?
- How can I find wholeness?

Chapter Three

From Your Peace to Theirs

Your Toolbelt for Peace

After you increase your own sense of peace, you can take the next step of setting the stage for peace in the classroom. Your attitudes and actions can create possibilities for peace. To encourage peaceable actions, you can develop a toolbelt for peace that includes these approaches:

- Using *I* language
- Modeling a win/win approach
- Teaching children to affirm themselves and others
- Teaching decision making, communication skills, and responsibility
- Encouraging neighborliness and listening

First of all, be an example. Your most powerful tool is the apprenticing you do as you model peaceable behavior. You train children through your own interactions and win/win approaches and by promoting their acceptance of self and neighbor.

When you speak about a problem, use *I* language. For instance, as children arrive at afterschool care, they are excited about starting games and often get noisy. A teacher might be tempted to say, "Can't you ever keep quiet? Stop that shouting!" (These comments label the children as shouters who are incapable of keeping quiet. Why should they try?)

Instead, the teacher, using *I* language, might say, "I can't concentrate when there's shouting. Let's remember to use indoor voices." Or, "I like it when we remember our classroom rules about noise." (These comments are less likely to lead to blaming one another and more likely to create motivation to live up to rules that are achievable.)

Your second tool for peacemaking is modeling a win/win approach. You make sure everyone wins when you do the following:

- Have a cooling-off time when there is a disagreement. Anger is intimidating and blocks solutions.
- Insist that all parties use *I* language when talking about the problem. Blaming blocks resolution.
- Have the children summarize what the other person said. This necessitates listening instead of tuning out each other to plan the next comment.
- Have each person take some responsibility ("I did…" or "I will…"). This defuses anger and leads to cooperation.
- Help participants brainstorm a variety of solutions. If you stop at the first workable solution, you may miss a creative approach that may energize true cooperation and change.
- Choose a solution everyone can agree on.
- End positively.

When you seek solutions that everyone can agree on, you have to make sure that everyone has input. For instance, suppose that some children on the preschool playground want to run, while others want to use the trucks and shovels to dig and pile up bark. When some children run through the bark piles, conflicts occur.

As you lead some problem solving (described in more detail in Chapter 10), suppose that the class chooses to alternate days for different activities. Monday, Tuesday, and Thursday would be digging days, and Wednesday and Friday would be running days. Your work is not over until you make sure that everyone is satisfied with the solution. You might notice, for instance, that Hal looks unhappy and do the following:

Teacher: "Hal, I notice that this solution doesn't appeal to you. You look unhappy. Can you tell us why?"

Hal: "I like to run, but I come on Tuesday and Thursday."

Teacher: "That means you would never get to run. Hal, do you have ideas on what would help so that you can do something you like to do?"

Hal: "Maybe I could run before they get out the truck box."

Another child: "After that, you could be our messenger." Hal looks interested.

Teacher: "Say more about that."

Child: "We need a runner between where we dig and our mountain. Hal could do that." Hal nods.

Now you have demonstrated a win/win approach. Does it work? If you follow the procedure, it does. You cannot take shortcuts and have it work.

One teacher stated at a group training that sometimes she cannot find a win/win approach. If she has to take a toy away during outside play because of misuse, another group of children sometimes wants the toy. No matter what she does, one group thinks she is unfair. They do not like any of the options she gives. What do you think is the problem?

Did your answers include the following?

• Children will be more likely to find a satisfactory solution if they come up with the possible solutions themselves. At present, they are rejecting the teacher's solutions.

• Persistence is crucial for problem solving. If none of the solutions is agreeable to everyone, you have to go through the process again. Do not cave into one group's persuasion. No one plays until all agree on a solution. Eventually, consensus occurs.

A final area in which your behavior affects peace is the feedback you give. Do not evaluate efforts as good. Instead, describe what is worth praising and how you feel: "I notice everyone kept working despite the loud noise outside. I feel proud that our class knows how to use time wisely." Commenting on behavior gives children a goal to work toward.

Affirm Self and Neighbor

You teach peacemaking by demonstrating it in your behavior, but you can also teach children specific skills of their own. The first peace skill you teach children should be how to treat themselves and others. It is important to teach them that peacemakers care about themselves and other people. They like who they are. They know that others are different than they are, but they still value others' special characteristics and talents.

These emphases come from two Bible verses: "You shall not take vengeance or bear a grudge against any of your people, but you shall love your neighbor as yourself: I am the LORD" (Leviticus 19:18). "You shall love the Lord your God…and your neighbor as yourself" (Luke 10:27).

You can help the children focus on loving neighbors as themselves by using activities that teach about accepting differences (pages 21–25).

When you teach children how to affirm themselves, you are also working on preliminary skills for peacemaking. We have to feel at peace inside in order to work on peace with neighbors. That inner sense of peace is blocked when a person feels unworthy and unable to do anything right, which is called low self-esteem.

Lovable, Capable, and Worthy

You can boost self-esteem by helping children feel lovable, capable, and worthy. First, act so that the children feel lovable. Communicate love in concrete forms: actions, expressions, words. Let them know you value each of them. Tell them they are a unique creation, and point out and treasure their characteristics: "Jane, your laugh is infectious; it makes us feel happy to hear you."

Children feel lovable when you give them individual attention, even for little portions of time. Make eye contact and respond to their needs when they tell you something. Children also feel more lovable when you accept them for who they are.

Help the children feel capable. Mark and record accomplishments in church, school, sports, or any venue. Praise the children's efforts: "Ray and Bill were honored at the Scout gathering. Tell us about the award you got." "Sally was determined to make the team. We're proud of her work." "Jasmine comes early each week to set out the choir folders on the chairs. That takes dedication."

Show that you value children's opinions and feelings: "I think it would help us live out our faith if we had a service project. Do you have ideas about people we could help?"

Encourage the children as they learn to play a musical instrument or sport, or give them an opportunity to use such skills in class. Encourage them to try their best. Communicate to elementary children that you are certain they are able to resolve their disagreement about sharing toys, games, or supplies. (Stay out of it and abide by their compromise.) Show that you think they are able to make decisions.

Even small actions and nuances make a person feel worthy—or unworthy. Watch what your tone of voice communicates. Do your words carry intonations of patience, disgust, powerlessness, expectation, sarcasm, trust, or distrust? What about the words others use in your classroom? Insist on dignity and respect for all.

Keep the child and his or her behavior separate, especially when making comments about inappropriate behavior. Do not say, "Sally, you're being cruel." Do say, "Sally, teasing Sharon is cruel."

Children feel worthy when you spend time conversing with them, when you encourage them, and when you remember what interests or concerns they had last week. Rules that provide boundaries also let them know that they are worth the trouble.

What Else Teaches Peace?

You can give children practical helps for getting along. The tips below will lead to a more peaceful classroom:

- Design and model a process of decision making. The children will copy it. Show them how to gather information, view all sides, weigh consequences and pros and cons, and then make a choice and stick with it.
- Take personal responsibility for your own duties and mistakes. Ask them to be responsible for theirs.
- Give them chances to help other people, for we meet God through helping others.
- Teach communication skills: how to listen, how to describe a problem, and how to find common ground.
- Teach neighborliness. Help them with social skills, especially in making friends, and point out how they can make and keep friends. Tell them that when they refer to people they help, they should use neighbor language: "neighbors" rather than "the needy" or "poor people."
- Teach children how to affirm one another's gifts. Start by giving a name to children's positive actions: "You bagged up all the recycling and threw away the trash. That's what I call helpful (or organized, or thoughtful, or neat)!" Encourage them to affirm one another's positive actions as well.

Encourage Listening

Listening is not always easy. Have you ever attended a lecture when the speaker was not quite loud enough? After awhile it gets hard to pay attention because you have to work so hard to listen. Be sure you acknowledge good listening when it happens.

Schools work on listening for reading readiness, but children also need peaceable listening skills. They can learn to truly focus on someone who is talking and to give nonverbal encouragement (nods, smiles). They can also make sure they understand others and have been understood. To find out what kind of listeners the children in your class are, play a listening game with them. Try "Me Riddles," "Name the Sound," or "This Is Me Bag" (pages 22–23). Note whether it was easy or hard for the children to listen. If listening is not easy for them, add listening games into your lesson plans.

Practicing listening pays off. First, the better the children listen, the more effective your teaching is. Also, when the children get ready to resolve conflicts, they will need to listen to one another's descriptions of what happened and to hear and understand all the possible solutions. Practice at listening is practice for conflict resolution. If you do not have extra time to develop listening skills, you can do it along with your lesson:

- When you need to have a movement break, use activities that require listening. For instance, have the children follow your instructions: "Brittany, stand up. Nicole, pat Jorge on the hand. Boys, turn around in place. Greg, jump up and down."
- Read a story that has a secret or a process, and afterward give the children a similar task to do. For example, read the story of Jesus' trip to the temple and his family's search for him. Have the children act out the sequence of actions to find Jesus.
- Before you tell a story, say, "Listen to find out..."
- Take the class on a listening field trip. Say, "Keep quiet so that you can hear every sound." With younger children, pause often to let the children name the sounds they have heard.
- Let the children take turns bringing a "This Is Me Bag" (page 23) to class. This bag gives listening practice and boosts self-esteem.
- Play a game where children can speak only if they are tossed the beanbag. Tell a story one sentence at a time and toss the bag before asking a question. "Jesus was going to Samaria. (*toss bag*) Where was he going? (*The child who caught the bag answers 'Samaria' and tosses the bag back to you.*) On the journey he was thirsty. He waited at the well. (*toss bag*) Where did he wait? (*at the well*) His disciples went into town to buy food. Where did they go?" (*into town*) Tell the rest of the story in this way.

Other listening activities include clapping games, music with movements, stories, fingerplays and poems, and reading short books without pictures. With younger children, have them listen to the sounds made as they drop coins into offering containers. During talk times, let the children take turns finishing one another's sentences as they retell the story. With older children, discuss problems and preferences and play guessing games. All of these exercise the children's listening muscles.

Listening and Respect

My mother taught for more than thirty years and still tutors elementary children. She and I agree that listening is the key to developing rapport with your students, and respect is a close second. Mom says that many of her successes as a teacher were because she treated children and their parents with respect. After all, when there is a problem, attacking creates a defensive posture in others.

When you respect other people, you also release the burden of trying to make them into someone else. You meet them where they are. When you approach others with respect and are willing to listen, you can usually find common ground even when you disagree. Often, you discover how God has been at work before you were.

Plan and Practice

Plan ahead to act more peaceably in your classroom. Write out examples of *I* language you could use in these situations:
- You find the class has misbehaved while your attention was elsewhere.
- Two children are struggling over a toy that must be shared.
- Two children will not pay attention and keep whispering in the back of the room.
- A child keeps making cute remarks that interrupt your presentation of the lesson.

Think about how to incorporate new techniques into your time with the children. Decide where and how you could promote higher self-esteem. Define moments when you might use a win/win approach.

Try It Out

The following activities are designed to help the children develop self-esteem and appreciation for their own gifts and the gifts of others. Consider including one of these activities in each class session.

Wanted Posters (elementary)

Materials: paper, felt-tip markers
Directions: Have the children write in large letters the word *Wanted* on a piece of paper. Then have them write in normal-sized letters some facts about themselves: name; height; hair color and length; what they like to do; favorite color; afterschool activity, sport, or hobby.

Bend and Shape (upper elementary)

Materials: pipe cleaners or small balls of modeling dough

Directions: Ask the children to take some quiet moments to shape the pipe cleaners or modeling dough. Use one of the phrases below to give participants something to think about while they shape an image to reflect what they are thinking:

- Something that reminds you of God
- Something that you are praying about to God
- Something that you think of when you think about Jesus
- Something that tells about you
- Something that you plan to do so that there is more peace around you

Me Collage (all ages)

Materials: magazines, glue, paper, pencils, and scissors

Directions: Have the children draw a simple outline of a person. Ask them to cut or tear out five or six pictures from magazines and to glue them in the outline. Tell them that the picture should remind them of, or describe, things they do or have in their family or home. Say, "For instance, if you have a dog, maybe you can find a picture of a dog. The dog may not look like your dog, but it will be a reminder that you have one. Maybe you could choose a picture of skates to say that you like skating. A picture of four people can stand for the four people in your family. Or you could draw your family. A picture of a CD can prompt you to tell us what kind of music you like. The aim is for you to make a collage and to be able to use it to tell about yourself."

Give elementary children eight to ten minutes to find and glue pictures. Younger children will need more time and help. About two minutes before they should finish, tell them to glue any remaining pictures and then to begin telling about their creation.

If your group has more than eight people, divide into groups of from four to six so that everyone has plenty of time to talk.

Note: While they are working is a good time to listen to each child. They will enjoy the personal interest.

Me Riddles (elementary)

Materials: large index cards (several per person), pencils or felt-tip markers, tape or tacks

Directions: Give each child an index card. Have the children fold it in half and write their name on the inside. Ask them to draw on the outside a picture of themselves doing something they like to do and to write a clue so that people can guess to whom the card belongs. The clue should be something another child might have heard about him or her, such as "collects baseball cards," "enjoys being in band; plays a trumpet," or "loves to go camping." The children can write two clues instead of drawing a picture if they wish. They can also make several cards, including one as a challenge card that even their friends may not know. Post the riddles so that the children have to lift the flap to see who fits the riddle.

Name the Sound (all ages)

Materials: tape recorder, blank tape

Directions: Record sounds for children to identify, such as a squeaking door, cabinets shutting, coffeepot gurgling, footsteps, dogs barking, and so forth. Keep a list of what you have recorded.

Play the tape in class. Allow the children to make several guesses for each sound; then tell them what the sound is.

This Is Me Bag (preschool and younger elementary)

Materials: sturdy paper or canvas bag, plain paper bag

Directions: Choose a sturdy paper or canvas bag. Send the bag home with a one child. Say to that child, "Bring five things that will help us know about you. For instance, the things you like to do, who is in your family, what is in your room." Explain the activity to the child's parent when you send the bag home. During the next class, let the child show each item in the bag and name what it stands for. Place the items back in the bag. Can the children recall what is in the bag? (Probably so.) If not, give hints or show any forgotten items to remind them of what was said about that child. Or repeat the show and try again. After class send the emptied bag home with a different child. (Put the items that the child brought in a plain paper bag to take home.)

Praise Notes (all ages)

Materials: bright copy paper or card stock, magazine pictures, glue

Directions: Make praise notes using the phrases below. For nonreaders, you may want to paste on pictures from magazines of people being kind, helpful, cheerful, or friendly. Use the praise notes yourself, and make some available to children to give to others when they see them doing good.

• You kept at it. That's persistence!
• Unique work!
• I like your cheerful spirit!
• You're friendly!

- Thanks for helping me. That was thoughtful!
- You are kind.
- You listened to me. That's the kind of friend I need.
- I could tell you listened to instructions. I appreciate that.
- You worked with us to get it done. That's cooperation!

Affirmation Badges (elementary)

Materials: crayons, white stick-on nametags

Directions: Have each child make a badge for him or herself. Tell the children to pick a positive characteristic they have and to write or draw the characteristic on a nametag. You may want to talk about possibilities first: friendly, kind, forgiving, funny, creative, talented dancer, and so forth. Have the children wear the badges during class.

Like Me (preschool and elementary)

Materials: crayons or felt-tip markers, paper

Directions: Line the children up. Let one child be the leader and stand across the room from the other children. The leader gets to tell things about him or herself: "I have two dogs." Anyone else who can say, "Like me" can move forward one step. The leader continues, "I like swimming" or "I am a big sister." Anyone who can say, "Like me" moves up each time, until someone reaches the leader. This is the new leader for another round.

With older children, divide the group into four teams and send them to the four corners of the room. Give each team paper and crayons or felt-tip markers. Have them select a runner. Say, "List three or four things describing yourself. The leader stands in the middle of the teams and says one thing at a time, such as "I like basketball." If you have "basketball" written on your sheet, you can send the sheet of paper to the leader and get a point. The runner has to bring the sheet of paper. Don't run to the leader individually—only one runner per team."

Pick a leader. Play until a team has eight points; then make that entire team the leader for the next round.

People Concentration (elementary)

Materials: photograph of each child brought from home, or instant camera to take a snapshot of each child, or paper and crayons for drawing self-portraits

Directions: Turn the photos or pictures face-down. To play, players turn over two pictures. If they can name any matching characteristics in the two pictures (such as height, smile, hair color, gender, hair length, and so forth), they keep the match. When all matches are made, play is over.

Same and Different Cards (elementary)

Materials: index cards, felt-tip marker

Directions: On each index card, write one descriptions, such as same hair color, different hair color, same height, different height, same eye color, different eye color, favorite foods, different gender, same number of brothers or sisters, same favorite game. Put the cards face-down in a pile.

To play: Have players take turns drawing cards. Whatever the card reads, the child tries to name a person who fits the description when compared with him or her. If players can name someone, they stay in the game. When everyone but one person has been eliminated, start again. Repeat five times. If you run out of cards, shuffle them to form a new pile.

Chapter Four

Setting the Stage for Peace

What Does It Look Like?

What does a peaceful classroom look like? First, the class and teacher have exciting, interesting things to learn together. Most of the time things go smoothly, though not always as planned. The desired outcome is not good behavior or children who can parrot back answers. Ephesians 4:15 gives us our goal: "But speaking the truth in love, we must grow up in every way into him who is the head, into Christ."

Second, in the peaceful classroom the teacher has a bag of tricks: ways to keep children focused, interested, and involved, with plenty of backup activities in case one does not work. Because their muscles need to move, the children move around in supervised learning games and drama or at free will to learning centers.

Third, in the peaceful classroom children know they are loved and appreciated. They feel capable and worthy and, with the teacher's help, act with respect for others. With help, they work together on projects without hurting feelings or excluding others.

It is not necessarily quiet, for the hum of activity can be heard. Occasionally, someone will say something such as, "I can't believe there are so many children in here."

Plan for Peace

Your planning can create this peaceful class as you increase children's participation and foster smooth transitions between activities. Lessons will go better when you have put in effort before the children arrive. It is similar to a stage show: You set the stage and rehearse responses and techniques. You arrange the room and the flow of what happens. Then, the players enter. The difference is that the children are not an audience to learning; they are the actors who make the lesson come alive.

Minimize Disruptions

One key to a peaceful class is to minimize disruptions. Some disruptions happen in classes when there is a mismatch between activities and either the interests or the abilities of students. Teachers who know the various ways children learn can teach with variety, which results in better discipline.

Other disruptions happen when you have not prepared. That is when things often go awry, or you cannot think of how to adapt activities when they do not go as intended. You feel frazzled and forget your purpose. You can create a more peaceful class by preparing. As you prepare, include techniques in this chapter. Incorporate them into your plan until they become routine.

You can also reduce discipline problems by the way you set up the room and operate. However, your objective should not be just to avoid discipline problems. You are forming community and teaching the limits for behavior. Children need boundaries, and they even test to see where they are. A friend once said, "Just because you put up a fence doesn't mean your job is over. What makes you think they won't test to see if it is still there?" You, as the adult, set the limits that create a feeling of security, comfort with exploration, and trust. Peace cannot happen without these.

Start Right

The peaceful classroom depends heavily on what happens at entry, whether children are involved in activities and able to move, and how music is used. In a peaceful classroom, there is a smooth flow from one activity to the next.

Perfect the flow of your lessons by first focusing on what happens as children arrive. Is there a lag while you wait on latecomers? Are you late yourself, and the children are already out of control when you arrive?

Here is how to solve many of your problems at entry: Be there early, and begin teaching the moment the first child walks in the door. Do not wait for the last child to enter or for everyone to quiet down. (By then, you will have lost most of the advantage of planning.) Keep the children focused on the main thing from the beginning.

Offer choices. Have a parent ready to tell a story or to play a tape with early preschool arrivers. The parent can go to an adult class once the rush of arrival is over.

If you have a child who is reluctant to enter, give the child some attractive choices of activities. This changes the question from "Won't you come in?" to "Which exciting thing do you want to do?" Always try to let children exercise control over choices (as long as they are choices you can accept). It gives them appropriate power and puts the focus on something besides entering.

For instance, invite preschoolers as they enter to choose between modeling dough, crayons, or the new (and thus interesting) dress-up clothes. Older children may begin a writing assignment or work a puzzle. Put several children to work on a skit or craft to present later. Let their project reinforce the lesson.

Involve Everyone

Make sure you involve everyone in learning. If you let some children check out, others will follow. The more student participation you have, the better their attention and retention are. For example, have them add sound effects for the Bible story or pose expressions of characters in the story.

Find out about your students' world and their faith. Ask what they already know about God and the church. What are their questions? What are their insights? Vary the learning activities so that all learners can enjoy something: a drama, a puzzle, or a game that lets less-verbal students shine.

Give every child a job. Even in the youngest classes, one child can straighten teacher materials; another can get supplies ready; someone else can separate and hand out the leaflets. After all, our goal is for each one to grow to his or her potential. Appropriate responsibility creates growth.

Allow Movement

Remember that the children are growing, so they have more trouble sitting still than adults do. Developing muscles need to move, and attention depends on comfort. Incorporate some wiggle breaks (stretching and movement) into your time together. For example, after intense concentration, play a teaching game that lets the children move muscles. Let them toss a ball as they repeat the Bible verse or other key thought. Label one wall "yes" and the opposite wall "no." Pose a variety of questions that can be answered with a yes or no, and let the students respond by moving to the appropriate wall. Play a relay game to grab word cards off a bulletin board and spell a Bible verse. Play musical chairs, with all children having to name a person from the Bible story before they can sit down.

Create transitions between activities. After a hectic activity, do something to relax and calm the children. Take deep breaths or sing a rousing song, then a quieter one.

If everyone seems bored or disinterested, take your teaching outside. Go on real or imaginary field trips around the church or even away from the building. Teach the same concepts but in a different space. Use the world as your classroom.

Play Is Important

Allow the children to show their natural exuberance. Play is their work. Why should we be surprised when we fail in our endeavors to get them not to play? Make play a part of the learning experience. When you teach about the Israelites packing up and moving, add a suitcase to the kindergarten home area. Play a ball game to learn a short Bible story: Whoever catches the ball has to tell something that happened in the story. Hide the words that form the Bible verse or that tell the lesson's theme; then have the children search for them. Play the game "I spy" using props that pertain to the lesson. Playing learning games works well for older children as well as for younger ones.

Use Your Whole Time

Have puzzles or other learning games on hand for times when the lesson ends early. Let the children keep journals, or give them *Pockets* (a children's devotional magazine published by the Upper Room) or other

Christian children's magazines to look at after assignments are completed. During the last five minutes of class, let the children play on computers or with Christian games. (Ask for donations of these items.) You have only forty-five minutes or an hour, compared with hours children spend watching television and using computers. Use all your time.

Use Peripheral Learning

A person's brain is constantly taking in and sifting messages from the environment. Take a look at the messages in your room. Does an out-of-season Christmas tree say that nothing has happened since then? Do pictures, charts, and posters carry out the lesson's themes? You can increase learning with posters and bulletin boards. Display posters that use Bible verses or other sayings about peace.

Use Music

Music recharges and re-energizes the brain and creates group feeling. Use music whenever you can: Play soft music while the children are working, or have them sing a song that reinforces the lesson. Songs help children remember the ABC's, so why not use them for Bible stories? Use songs for instructions: "It's time to pick up our toys" (to the tune of "Hickory Dickory Dock"). Use songs for worship. Think how often the Psalms include the words *I will sing*. Music is an important part of worship and a powerful communication tool.

Plan for Leaving

Prepare the children for leaving near the end of the class session. Many children will need closure, a time to finish their artwork or activity before parents arrive. Explain what you will be doing in the last ten minutes: "We're going to color greeting cards for an ill classmate until parents arrive" or, "You have ten minutes to work on your skits for next week."

Young children may get upset as other children's parents pick them up, wondering where their own parents are. To minimize disruption, face the children away from the door. With any age group, choose an ending activity that does not rely on numbers of participants to work. Some good choices are singing, storytelling, reading a book, individual art (not murals), and telling personal stories.

Establish Routines

Children need structure, so help them by providing routines that let them know how to behave in specific situations. Do this by teaching the children regular routines for entering and leaving the room, for conversation, and for how refreshments and materials are distributed. For instance, when it is time to leave, clean up your area and then line up at the door to receive your papers and notes to go home. One person a week helps hand out cups and napkins while another hands out cookies. The teacher pours the drinks, and everyone else stays seated.

Pay particular attention to transition times, when children are changing activities or are coming and going. Some children need a few minutes' warning that it is almost time to stop playing or to finish artwork. Others finish early and bounce around the room if a transition activity has not been planned.

Here are some examples that announce coming transitions:
- "Everyone who is finished, go with Ms. Rashonda to collect leaves outside for our next activity."
- "Those who are waiting can use the modeling dough at the table. The rest of us need to finish our story in three minutes."
- "Mr. Jones is ready to sing with us. If you are finished, go on to the circle rug while the rest of us finish up the pictures."

Plan ahead for these transition times:
- Circle time (for younger children)
- Arrival of the music leader
- Arrival of parents to pick up children
- Changing from a large-group activity to a small-group activity or learning centers

Use Signals

Signals are great tools. Use them as a shorthand for words and as a way to save your voice. Some are most effective when reserved for occasional use. I remember from grade school, for example, that lowered lights meant that we had misbehaved and were about to be reprimanded. Once, the teacher used the signal when we were working quietly, and it got everyone's attention. She had something important to tell us and used novelty to make sure we were paying attention. If lowered lights are used routinely, however, students begin to ignore them.

Other signals combined with a routine can shape behavior. For instance, in the hubbub of chatter, say softly, continuing until everyone has joined in: "If you can hear me, clap your hands." Change your directions as children join you, "If you can hear me, touch your ear." "If you can hear me, snap." Keep giving directions until all are participating. When all have joined in, introduce the next activity immediately. A similar routine is to clap a pattern and see if children will match it. Vary the pattern and make it harder so that everyone will have to listen to participate. While they are concentrating on you is a great time to launch into what you need to tell them.

Ask your class to help develop and practice signals. A raised hand could mean, "Be quiet. Raise your own hand." The stop hand signal that a traffic officer might use could mean to "freeze." Cup your hands behind your ears to signal the need to listen. Ring a bell for quiet. When children whine or shout, touch your ears to indicate, "I can't hear you until a proper voice is used." Nonverbal cues can be more powerful than words at the same time that they minimize interruptions. Let the children suggest signals you can use, for this empowers them as well by making them part of the decision-making process.

In the Know

Jeremiah 7:23 says, "Obey my voice, and I will be your God, and you shall be my people; and walk only in the way that I command you, so that it may be well with you." We become a people through our obedience to God. It is important to maintain that sense of community, of being a people together with a certain way of doing things. Some of those things are important lifestyle choices, such as obeying the Ten Commandments. Others are smaller ways that mark how we belong.

Create a sense of belonging by having some rituals and routines unique to your class. A countdown routine is an example: 5–Hug yourself. 4–Blink at me. 3–Pat your head. 2–Reach up high. 1–Put your hands in your lap. Teach the routine and practice it. Use the routine for one function only, such as for time to go. Practice it and say what the children should do as you demonstrate. Eventually, you can count 5-4-3-2-1 and the children will do the routine without your reminder. A countdown routine, like other class signals or routines, functions as a group-building tool because it is a mystery to outsiders but familiar to the class.

Other tools that create belonging are a class prayer or song. For younger children, choose a one- or two-sentence prayer and one song for grace at snacks. Help older children write a prayer or song to use week after week in closing, and have several meal graces to choose from.

Schedules and Rules

If your elementary class keeps asking, "When is class over?" they may not be bored; they may just need to have the schedule posted. Even grownups like to know where they are headed and if they are almost there. Lay out what you expect to do during the session, and let the children know how the lesson time is progressing.

Often, we wrongly assume that children know our expectations for them during Sunday school. Some have never been to Sunday school before. Others have attended childcare in the very rooms we use but with a whole different set of rules. You need to explain what you expect.

Post the rules on a poster or chalkboard. Three to five rules is plenty, as the list needs to be short enough to remember. Talk with the class about the consequences of breaking the rules. What happens when someone pushes another, for instance? What will appropriate responses be when someone breaks a rule?

Have a teaching plan for each behavior you expect:
- Explain what you expect.
- Put it in writing.
- Demonstrate it.
- Have the students practice it.

For example, one rule might be, "Use walking feet when we go down the hall." The teacher explains that walking feet means you do not run, skip, or hop; you walk. The teacher writes out the rule or points it out on a poster. The teacher demonstrates walking feet, and then has the children practice around the room or even down the hall and back. Afterward, when children are running down the hall, a leader has only to call, "Walking feet," and the children know exactly what is expected.

Also, be sure to tell them your expectation that they will benefit from values and concepts in the lesson. Let them know the reasons you teach them. (You think their lives will be better; you want them to learn the Christian way; you want them to know Jesus; and so forth.)

Does this seem too complicated for Sunday school or fellowship groups at church? Think about routines or structures you already use. Don't your children know exactly how long they can ignore you before they have to get quiet? Your voice and demeanor are unwitting signals.

With your preschool group, do you already sing, "It's time to clean up; it's time to clean up for story time"? That is a clean-up signal and a ritual. Do you dim the lights when it is time for students to listen to the Bible story? That is a signal that helps focus attention on listening. If you incorporate some new techniques, you might smooth out your class time, maximize your productive time, and minimize discipline problems.

Teach the Whole Child

Find a way for each child, even challenging ones, to be admired and recognized, even if it is for sharing decorations from home or bringing snacks. You might try a "We Are Great!" bulletin board, where children can post photographs from home or sports ribbons. Make sure that even the least-noticed child has something on the board. Such recognition helps children believe that they are appreciated and capable.

Foster friendships in the classroom between children and with you. We need community as much as we need knowledge. Do not limit yourself to imparting information, for spiritual formation requires listening as well as talking. Sometimes we learn as much from children as they learn from us.

Be aware of age-level abilities and life issues so that you can keep your teaching relevant to your students' lives. Talk to children, read their magazines or books, and check out their media.

Examine Interactions

Think about the interactions between people in your classroom. Children interact with you and your helpers and with one another. What attitudes do you observe?

Evaluate your time together. Are you treating children fairly? Psalm 99:4 calls God a "lover of justice." Fairness is an important part of a peaceful classroom. Do you call on children equally? Also, when problems develop, have you taken children aside to talk privately? Children need the same respect we give adults.

Think about your reward system. Rewards for learning or behavior can be what some educators call emotional poison to the brain. They teach that learning and acceptable behavior are not enough on their own but must be paid for. Praise can limit learning when it seems too fulsome or empty or imparts a burdensome perfection to measure up to. Children respond best when you acknowledge their achievement: "Antion, you made every meeting of the junior greeters. I am proud of your reliability."

Do not set yourself up as the time-out police. Instead, help your children motivate themselves. Guide them to set goals, and mark their progress. Point out and celebrate when they have achieved their goals. Help the children want to behave; foster their internal motivation, and they will continue behaving well, even when there is not an enforcer. Here are some less tangible rewards that might help build motivation and help the children see themselves as leaders:

- Being the helper
- Being the line leader
- Getting free time for snacks or talking
- Having a turn taking home a cassette or CD of Christian music
- Getting to choose the next activity for the class
- Having time to read *Pockets* or other children's periodicals
- Receiving a free devotional magazine
- Having a party when the whole class has met a goal

Expand Your Resources

When you do not know how to address a situation, talk to an experienced Sunday school teacher or to a public school teacher in your community. Most are willing to talk about what works for them or to let you observe them in action. If you follow their advice with no results, you might even try trading classes with another Sunday school teacher for a few weeks. Sometimes personalities react differently with different people. The visiting teacher may be able to provide new insights and suggestions.

Recruit a prayer partner. As you tell your prayer partner about children who are particularly challenging, be specific about what is needed: help in overcoming distractions or a child who needs success, for instance. Spend a few minutes together praying for those children and for God to work through you to bring grace to the children in your care. People brought the children to Jesus so that he could pray for them (Matthew 19). We can do likewise.

Expect to receive from as well as to give to the children. Listen to them so that you can be rewarded by the marvel of God's work in them. You will discover that you are not alone, that God is there with you. If you tend your class with prayer, respect, and concern for the needs of the children, God will greatly increase what you sow.

This chapter's tips and techniques are not only about classroom management but also about peace skills. As you lay a foundation of classroom management, you show that you have the ability and authority to teach peace.

Try It Out

Here are some poster ideas for your classroom. Post them to help with peripheral learning.

Conflict Resolution Guidelines (all ages)

Materials: posterboard and felt-tip marker

Directions: Write the following on a large piece of paper and post it so that everyone can see it.

- Respect one another.
- Listen when someone is talking. Do not interrupt.
- Be honest, but do not blame or call names.
- Think of as many solutions as you can.
- Choose a solution everyone agrees with.
- End positively: Say something nice about the other person, or ask for or express forgiveness.

Feelings Chart (all ages)

Materials: posterboard, felt-tip markers, glue, magazines or instant camera

Directions: Write these words on a poster, leaving space for drawing or pasting faces that show these expressions. Classes can make their own charts by posing and taking instant photographs or finding pictures in magazines.

- anxious
- confused
- sad
- excited
- scared
- content
- relaxed
- tired
- frustrated
- worried
- bored
- furious
- angry
- safe
- happy
- lonely

Position Yourself for Peace (all ages)

Materials: large piece of paper, felt-tip marker

Directions: Write the following on a large piece of paper and post it so that everyone can see it.

P ractice, kindness.

O bserve how others feel.

S olve problems, even when it is hard.

I f you do wrong, make it right.

T hank others.

I f you're talking with someone, take turns.

O nly speak positive things about others.

N otice what is unique about others.

F orgive someone who wrongs you.

O nly say what you feel; use *I* language.

R espect other people.

P ostpone talking until you have cooled down.

E xpress how you feel with words.

A ccept yourself for who you are.

C elebrate the differences in people.

E liminate blaming.

Chapter Five

Roots of and Responses to Misbehavior

Proverbs 12:1 says, "Whoever loves discipline loves knowledge." The writer knew the importance of disciplining yourself for learning. After all, *disciple* and *discipline* are related words. Discipline is both a learned way of behavior and a set of consequences for actions that break the rules of the group or impede learning. Discipline in the church setting needs to include consequences, or planned responses to misbehavior. Patterns of behavior, including misbehavior, were learned at some point or another. They can be unlearned through discipline. Be aware, however, of the difference between punishment and letting children suffer the consequences of actions. Punishment is a threat that shuts down thinking. Consequences may teach cause and effect.

There are times when any child misbehaves. How a person copes with misbehavior is critical, but Sunday school teachers are often unsure of what to do. Volunteer teachers are often hesitant to mete out consequences because they want to offer grace to students who rarely come to church or get little positive reinforcement elsewhere. Grace, however, may be found in requiring accountability from the children and in setting boundaries for behavior so that all can learn. Psalm 94:12-13 tells us, "Happy are those whom you discipline, O Lord, and whom you teach out of your law, giving them respite from days of trouble." Grace and discipline are intertwined.

Grace-filled discipline does not mean we shut down students who do not behave as we wish. It means we keep trying to reach them. As mentioned previously, undesirable behaviors are learned somewhere. The behavior would not continue if it did not reap the child a reward in some form. That reward might be prestige or attention, even negative attention such as scolding or punishment. Most children can learn to seek a different reward; that is, a positive affirmation for acceptable behavior.

It takes effort, however, to change. It takes effort, both on your part and on the part of the child. Part of your effort is to understand children and how they learn.

Roots of Misbehavior
Role of the Brain

When the scarecrow in *The Wizard of Oz* receives his brain, he suddenly spouts formulas and knowledge. Not quite so dramatically, the brain does indeed turn on or off the learning and acceptable behavior in your students.

The brain, as part of the body, is governed by all the cycles and rhythms that affect the body. Lack of water, oxygen, or protein makes it hard to learn; therefore, drinks of water and breaths of fresh air are important. And perhaps we should bring ham instead of doughnuts to Sunday school. Things such as lighting also make a difference in how children pay attention. The brain works best in natural light, less so in incandescent and fluorescent lighting.

Other factors influence the brain's response. Have you ever felt sluggish when it was too hot? or perked up when you smelled a fragrant citrus fruit or put on bright colors? I have a rainbow dress I wear when I feel low because it energizes me. Similarly, I painted my office in ocean hues because they were soothing to me. I later learned that blue and green are calming colors.

Lighting, water, oxygen, nutrition, color, and physical comfort all affect how the brain responds. As you teach, arrange your room or walls to enhance sensory input. We have already mentioned the peripheral images of posters on the wall, but also consider the lighting, plants, cleanliness, clutter, and music. Clutter distracts. Music calms or energizes. Evaluate the physical environment of your room. Does it enhance learning, or is it a detriment? Does the atmosphere say that exploration is okay? Have you taken care of physical needs that might interfere with attentive behavior?

Also remember that, just like the body's muscles, the brain gets tired. After focused concentration, the brain needs down time. Recall when you have listened carefully to a speaker, even one who is interesting. Your attention picks up with incidents that really touch your life. You listen closely, and then you find yourself drifting and thinking about other things. This is down time. You may or may not come to attention again, depending on whether you have maxed out your attention span or if your prime attention time has been used up by preliminary details. Sometimes there is just too much material to absorb. Do not let students reach overload before you get to important stuff. Really use the first minutes you have, since more people listen and focus then.

Stress Blocks Learning

You can present the best material in the best way, but a child who endures chronic stress or neglect will not have his or her brain engaged to learn. Stress and trauma—from abuse, neglect, violence, disaster, and even loss—cause the survival mechanisms of the brain to take control, often leading to increased impulsivity or aggression. When the brain recognizes that you are not safe or are frightened or overwhelmed, it deploys all resources to answering the threat and abandons work on less important activities.

Grief and loss can cause stress for children and affect their ability to learn. Many children experience grief through the death of a family member or pet, divorce, moving, or loss of friends.

Stress and trauma can block learning even after the stress is experienced. For example, when a child is beaten, the brain's survival mechanism is deployed. Rational thought is temporarily disengaged. Eventually, raised voices may cause the same response. Sometimes when a child has experienced panic over and over, the sense of threat never subsides, and clear thinking becomes difficult. The child is robbed of the opportunity to learn.

Responding to Misbehavior
What if the children will not sit still for the story?

Review your lesson plan to make sure you are not asking the children to sit for too long. Give the children chances to move and stretch during story time by adding sound effects and motions. You can even have a shorter story time, but have it twice. To roughly estimate children's attention span, add two to their age. That is how many minutes they can listen at one time. Not long, is it?

Since they can sit and listen for only short periods of time, find a way to communicate content through music, games, or drama. Sing the Bible verse. Act out what happened. Hide items relating to the story, and have the children search the room for them. As they find each one, tell them what the item means. Who says you have to sit down to learn something?

Affirm something about each child. We all listen better when the focus is on us. Include their names in stories when you can.

When children do not sit still, they may not be making a connection between the topic and their lives. Help them make the connection by incorporating their interests. If Lauren collects rocks, have her bring her collection when you tell the story of Peter being named Rock.

If everyone is hyped up, perhaps all you need is to provide transition between action and quiet.

What if children constantly interrupt?

Allow some time for the children to talk. When you are ready to start, say, "Now it's time for me to tell the story. Please listen without talking." If someone interrupts or talks to a neighbor while you're telling the story, incorporate the child's name into the story or put your hand on his or her shoulder. Bring attention back to the story by asking the interrupter a question: "Grace, how did Jesus' parents feel when he was missing?"

What if they push, shove, or grab toys?

Name the child's feelings: "It looks as if you're angry. That's okay, but hurting someone is not okay." Also, give some direction for what to do next, including ways to get what they want without hurting someone: "What can you do to feel better? Can you find a new toy to play with? ask Keesha to share? stomp your feet?"

With young preschoolers, you have to remind them to use their words. Give them appropriate words: "Kim, instead of hitting, say, 'No, I want to play with this toy alone.'"

Review the rules and redirect: "We don't kick other people. Would you like to play with the fire engine until Sammy is finished with the milk truck?" This works with older children as well, although you may ask them for ideas about redirecting their actions. With older children, you may need to say, "I know you can work out something. Solve this problem so that both of you are happy with the results."

Teach negotiation: "Ginger, maybe Keith will trade the car for this airplane." (Ginger may decide to keep the airplane herself. That is okay.) Teach the children how to get along as a group.

What if children whine or shout?

If you have a signal, such as touching your ear, use it and say, "I can't hear you when you speak in a whining voice." Express how you feel about the behavior, not the child: "I like to hear indoor voices. Shouting hurts my head." Or, "Whining irritates me."

State the rules and point out the consequences: "We do not shout. If you cannot use the race track without shouting, you will have to give me the racing car."

Praise the child while he or she is behaving as you want: "Yasmin, I like the way you're talking so quietly."

What if a child is disruptive and draws others into inappropriate behavior?

First, direct the child's leadership to positive ways. Give the disruptive child a legitimate position as leader or trainer. Next, make more leaders. You can do so by giving other children leadership in games or by placing them as captains or team leaders for work projects. The children will not be as swayed by the disruptive child if they can follow other leaders.

If these steps do not work and the child remains disruptive, ask the parent about approaches used at home. Or, if you are concerned about developmental or emotional problems, work with a church staff member to recommend a diagnostician. Do not recommend therapy or intervention without talking it over with a professional staff member, as the church may have policies or referral procedures you need to know about.

You may be afraid of hurting parents' feelings, but do not let that deter you from doing something. Consult with church staff or talk to the parents, but do something. Other children are often afraid of uncontrolled children. If you do not address the situation, you may end up losing class members because of one child. More importantly, the child may not get needed help without your honesty.

In one church, the custodial grandparents were surprised and a little defensive when the teacher suggested (after consultation with the child-care director and church staff) that they take their two-year-old for a diagnosis at the children's hospital. The grandparents assumed family upheaval was responsible for the child's delayed development. It turned out that the child was deaf, and the family ended up getting free remedial therapy and special schooling. They made a special trip to tell the teacher what she already knew: Intervention during preschool years can make the difference between success and struggle for an entire life of learning. They were grateful for her willingness to speak up.

Sometimes when you know a child has health or developmental problems, you may need to ask for an aide to work with that one child. One church asked a college student to work with Sandra on Sunday mornings as part of that student's internship. Another church hired an extra nursery worker to accompany Evan to Sunday school and stay with him whenever he was in church childcare. They felt the need to safeguard other children at the same time that they offered grace to the family of a chronically impulsive child.

If you think the problem is really on your end of things, and you just need more responses in your repertoire, you can ask another teacher to try his or her best to redirect the child. Sometimes another person can get different results or think of something new.

What if a child runs out of the room?

This is one reason to always have two adults in the classroom. You can find the child who left while another adult continues the class lesson. If you cannot leave the class, enlist help to find the child. Ask another teacher to let your class visit for a while, or find a Sunday school superintendent or other volunteer to search for the child. As a last resort, take the class with you. It is imperative to find a missing child.

When you do find the child, talk with the child privately. You will get better results if the child is not playing to a crowd. Also, there may be issues the child does not want to mention in front of others: feeling hurt, being upset about family issues, or feeling unaccepted.

Do not be afraid to approach the parent for help if the child repeats the behavior. Most parents will be cooperative when it comes to keeping their child safe.

What if the class seems bored?

This is an instance when it would be refreshing to take your lesson outside or to a different room. Teach about the sacraments in the room where the altar guild prepares the elements. Use a stairway as a temporary amphitheater for a story. Different perspectives renew zest for learning.

Re-examine your teaching plan any time learners seem bored. You may be teaching above or below their level or relying too much on one method of communication.

What if initial entry into the room creates problems?

With preschool classes in particular, entry can be a stressful time. Children balk at coming in, and parents get more and more stressed as they think about being late to their own class. They worry about the possibility that their child might cry the entire hour. Your first step is to reassure the parents. Find out where the parents will be, and let them know you will find them if their child cries continually.

You can decrease entry problems by offering calming sensory choices for preschoolers. Let them shape modeling dough, measure rice in and out of containers, or paint with water. Have music playing. Create interest with hands-on items from the stories you will be teaching. If you are telling about David, for instance, you might have a flock of stuffed sheep for early arrivers to play with. Tell children as they come to the door, "We're going to hear about a young shepherd who became a king. Would you like to play a shepherd with our sheep? Or you can make a sheep from modeling dough."

For elementary children, entry is easier if you help them form groups. Have a banner or poster that several can work on if they choose. Let some others choose props for a skit later in the class.

Teach teamwork. Give them a project and assign the different tasks needed to complete it. Tell them that you trust them to do their own portions, and then put them together. Also be aware that for some ages, girls may want to work in groups with girls and boys with boys.

Provide individual puzzles and art supplies for those who would rather work alone.

What if children are revved up?

Wonderful moments occur in class when children are enjoying intensely what is going on. Sometimes it is hard to get everyone calmed back down after there has been laughter, games, and suspense. It takes some intentional effort on your part.

First, help the students release energy. Have them give some pretend sighs from high to low notes. Tell everyone to shake all the wiggles out. Sing some songs. Start with high-energy songs and wind down to softer, slower ones.

Allow a few silly moments. Ask everyone to make a silly face at a neighbor. Then ask them to make a joyful face, an angry face, a sad face, and a listening face.

Use their energy. Have the children clean up their space. Change your lesson activity from a discussion to a body vote: "Move to the window if you agree that most people lie every day." "Move to the door if you agree that Jesus said it was okay to lie occasionally." "Move to the bulletin board if you agree that it's okay to lie to keep from hurting someone's feelings."

Help them calm down by using a countdown routine (similar to the one mentioned earlier to give a class a sense of belonging).

5. Reach up high.
4. Reach down low.
3. Stand up and sway.
2. Hands on waist.
1. Stand still in place.

A countdown that would use up the wiggles might be

5. Put your right foot in and out until I say it is time to stop.
4. Shake your head and keep your foot moving.
3. Stop moving your foot and head, but now jump in place.
2. Turn around while still jumping.
1. Shake the wiggles out and sit down.

What if children make fun of someone in the class?

Children need adults to state what is appropriate and to make everyone stick by the policy. If you have a rule that no one should call names or make fun of another person, do not ignore such comments. Restate the rule: "In this class we do not say anything about another person unless it is positive."

Make sure that those who make fun of others are removed from the attention their behavior gets them from classmates:

- Send them out with a helper to get supplies, to report attendance, or to separate them from the others for a moment.
- Talk to them privately, and ask them to consider how a person feels when someone makes fun. If they can remember being the object of jokes or name-calling, ask them to refrain from causing another person to feel that way.
- If they say, "Well, Andy made fun of me," respond, "So you know how belittling it is to be made fun of. I think I can trust you to build up our classmates, not to tear them down."
- If they say, "Sara was doing it, too," then respond, "I'm talking to you right now."

If you have a chronic problem with some children banding up and excluding others, plan to mix up the groups.

- Play a fruit basket game, which changes seating. Between every two or three rounds, have neighbors tell each other something about themselves.
- Play games that require collaboration, such as "Cooperation Game" and "A Foot at a Time" (page 49).

- Mix the groups further by setting up work groups to divide up a clique. Divide the groups to include some people who do not know one another. Give them a project that involves each person, such as making a poster, writing a skit about the story, or listing as many ways as possible that group members are like someone in the story.
- Spend some time on activities that help the children discover ways they are like one another. Play "Like Me" (page 24) or "People Concentration" (page 25).

You can also make a "We All Matter to God" montage. Have the children search magazines for pictures of people of various heights, ages, and appearances. Have them cut out the pictures and glue them on one poster. Talk about the variety of people God has chosen to create and love. Say, "We are all important to God. We need one another. What if everyone knew how to use computers and no one cooked? What if everyone played soccer and no one liked basketball? Our differences are gifts from God."

Teach them the following:
- Individuals are different on the outside, but inside they feel much the same as other people.
- Each person, wherever he or she lives and whatever language he or she speaks, needs food and clothes and a home. Everyone needs love.
- Our differences are what are special about us. Tell people how special they are.
- Peacemakers accept others for the way they are. You are just the way God meant you to be.
- Because we are different, we belong together. We are better because of one another.

You can also read stories about children who feel excluded or who learn to include others. Invite comments about how the characters in the story feel.

Disciples Have Discipline

Discipline is not about punishment; it is about you and your students learning a way to behave. That is what discipleship is: following a teacher and learning to act as the teacher counsels. As disciples of Christ, we are called to the discipline of love and peacemaking.

Teachers can benefit from these words to fathers about their children: "Bring them up in the discipline and instruction of the Lord" (Ephesians 6:4). Good discipline is a foundation for meaningful work, whether it is in a school setting or in Sunday school. The more you are ready to respond purposefully rather than react, the better you are poised to handle conflict when it happens.

As you work with children, though, keep in mind that they are less able than youth or adults to analyze themselves and their behavior. They often repeat what seems to adults to be the same behavior. Because they are not abstract thinkers and are still learning the concepts of cause and effect, sequencing, and chronology, they may not be able to apply the learning from one situation to another.

The more examples and practice you give the children, the more likely it is that they will respond peacefully when emotion is involved. Without careful forethought, the most frequented pathways in the brain are traveled, whether that pathway is lashing out, talking to others, or seeking harmony.

Our human minds are a complex and marvelous testament to the Creator. Our minds are a key to peace, and God has given us instructions on how our minds can be shaped in peaceable ways. Philippians 2:5 says, "Let the same mind be in you that was in Christ Jesus." Philippians 4:7 encourages: "And the peace of God, which surpasses all understanding, will guard your hearts and your minds in Christ Jesus." The Bible confirms what science now has explored: The roots of behavior and discipline are in the mind. As Christians, we find hope and direction in the example of Christ.

Try It Out

Here are some activities to help avoid cliques.

Cooperation Game (all ages)

Materials: two ropes or strings long enough to encircle the team

Directions: Divide the group into two teams. Give each team a rope or string. Have each team huddle up and then tie the rope around them. Make sure the teams are about equidistant from you. Say, "You are to move as a team to get to me. Move the way I tell you, holding onto the rope and without hurting anyone in your group or losing anyone. You have to arrive whole and healthy to get a point."

Tell the teams how to move, and then say, "Get ready. Get set. Go! Move backward."

After one team has reached you, repeat the game with (1) backward (again), (2) sliding, (3) crawling, (4) hopping.

A Foot at a Time (elementary)

Materials: three paper footprints per person (cut in advance or traced before the game)

Directions: Divide the group so that the teams face each other across the room.

Give each person three footprints. Tell the children that the first team to get across the room and then back to you is the winner. The only problem is that they may not step anywhere except on a paper footprint. Say, "Get ready. Get set. Go!"

Some players will probably move by using only their own footprints. Others will get with a friend and pool their footprints. Some may organize a group effort.

When the game is over, discuss how cooperation helped a team win.

Chapter Six

Creating the Best Fit

Discipline is less of a problem when there is a proper fit between abilities and activities, since human beings are designed to learn. Educators say that everyone can be intrigued with learning, if a proper fit is found.

Think about the methods of teaching you experienced when you were a child. Some methods made the material easy to understand, and others did not. If you learned to play an instrument, ride a horse, type, debate, or take photographs, each instructor probably used different methods.

Not all learning is by formal instruction. I first realized what a responsibility Mary had in rearing Jesus when, as a teenager, I played Mary in a Nativity pageant. In college I learned Isaiah's names for the Messiah by singing them with the choir. I still learn and recall many Bible verses by singing them. We tend to choose activities that allow us to learn the way we like to learn.

The challenge for teachers is to provide activities that intrigue a variety of individuals. Each child's brain is uniquely wired, which leads to different ways of learning. Learning is also determined by a child's developmental stage.

Cognitive Development

Children approach the world differently than adults do. From birth to two years of age, they learn by taking things in, usually by mouth. Through sensorimotor exploration, infants and toddlers develop the ability to remember absent objects. (Out of sight out of mind works for only a while.) They also experiment with cause and effect. (They drop an object off the highchair tray—again, and again, and again.) Although they remain naturally self-centered, toddlers gradually come to an understanding of self among other objects rather than the cause of all events.

When children are between the ages of two and seven, they develop spoken language and explore the workings of the world. They do not realize at first, for instance, that number, liquid, weight, and volume remain the same when an item is moved or is poured elsewhere. This is why they cannot understand that Sarah's sandwich that is cut into fourths is not more than Sammy's that is cut into halves. They think Sarah has four, so she has more than Sammy has. As they move blocks from one place to another, children are learning that eight blocks inside the box are the same as eight on the table or eight on the floor.

Between about seven to somewhere around eleven or twelve years of age, children are in a stage of concrete operations. They develop the ability to classify information and relate two or more facts, but their logic is still limited to concrete situations. They connect with and apply only what they see, hear, and experience, which is why they are called concrete thinkers. They do not understand abstract ideas.

Toward age eleven or twelve, children seem to reorganize thinking and do abstract thinking. For that reason, many churches have moved confirmation classes from upper elementary years to middle school and early adolescence, when more conceptual topics can be broached.

Multiple Intelligences

Educational researcher Howard Gardner asserts that the human mind is not one intelligence but a set of abilities. He believes there are a variety of types of intelligence. According to Gardner, the reason there is so much variety in learning and ability is that no two people have the same combination of intelligences and experiences. This means that people learn in different ways. Although everyone uses all the intelligences to some extent, most people are stronger in one or two.

Intelligences that Gardner has described include these:

- **Linguistic (verbal)**—People who are strong in this intelligence learn through words: reading, speaking, and listening. These learners like storytelling, poetry, word puzzles, and other learning activities that use reading and speaking. It is the intelligence most commonly used in teaching.

- **Logical-mathematical**—Besides mathematics, this intelligence deals with patterns and relationships between ideas. These learners are interested in learning steps and discovering how things develop. Logical-mathematical intelligence is employed in analysis, scientific investigation, statistical comparisons, and the study of maps and timelines.

- **Spatial (visual)**—Learners who are strong in this intelligence are able to visualize and create internal mental pictures. They are gifted at recognizing patterns in space and other arenas. Activities that use this intelligence include watching videos, drawing pictures, studying maps, and developing charts and graphs.

- **Musical**—Learners who favor this intelligence easily recognize, perform, and/or compose musical patterns. They are sensitive to tone, melody, rhythm, and timbre. The exercise of musical intelligence involves solving problems or creating products with music or rhythm. Use call and response songs, chants, tunes, and rhythms; have learners set Scripture to music; or choose and sing a hymn as a prayer.

- **Bodily-kinesthetic**—Learners strong in bodily-kinesthetic intelligence learn best through physical movement and the manipulation of objects. They like drama, posing, tracing with the finger, dance, and games that use movement.

- **Interpersonal**—This type of intelligence involves the ability to understand the intentions, motivations, and desires of others. People who are strong in this intelligence enjoy cooperative learning activities, discussions, and small-group projects.

- **Intrapersonal**—People strong in intrapersonal intelligence have a good understanding of themselves and are aware of their own fears, desires, and abilities. Reflection and silence come more easily to these learners. They like quiet time to apply new knowledge or experiences to their own lives. Activities such as journaling work well for them.

Applying the Theory

To the child who learns best through bodily-kinesthetic intelligence, the most detailed chart is not going to communicate as well as a chance to act out the scene. You can vary your approaches to involve multiple intelligences in learning. Decide which intelligence is engaged by each of the following learning activities. Some activities may involve more than one intelligence.

1. Hearing a story about Samuel and Eli
2. Acting out the story of the good Samaritan
3. Making up a news report about the meaning of the Pentecost events
4. Drawing a scene from the Bible story
5. Writing in a journal after each lesson
6. Charting the events of the Exodus
7. Seeing a video about baptism
8. Participating in Holy Communion
9. Making a video about Jesus' disciples
10. Handling props related to a Bible story (such as a mustard seed or sheep's wool)
11. Rhyming a version of the Ten Commandments
12. Tracing Jesus' journeys on a map
13. Creating instrumental sounds to convey the meaning of Psalm 23

Answers will vary. You might have listed the following intelligences:
1. Linguistic (verbal)
2. Bodily-kinesthetic
3. Linguistic (verbal), logical-mathematical, intrapersonal or interpersonal (depending on if it is an interview or an editorial)
4. Spatial (visual)
5. Intrapersonal
6. Logical-mathematical
7. Spatial (visual)
8. Bodily-kinesthetic, intrapersonal, interpersonal, linguistic (verbal)
9. Bodily-kinesthetic, spatial (visual), interpersonal
10. Spatial (visual)
11. Musical
12. Logical-mathematical
13. Musical

Read the following activities and determine which of your children would understand the lesson best through each method.
- A student pretending to be a character in the story and answering questions from classmates
- Children describing the meaning of "love your neighbor" by moving to music or finding pictures in books
- Groups working together to turn a Bible verse or story into a chant or cheer

- Children looking around the church with you for an opportunity to help someone
- All the class members cooperating to make a human sculpture that shows how to make disciples

Think about the techniques mentioned and ones you already use. Are there new methods you could incorporate that would reach certain children in your class? You will find that children who are engaged in activities that appeal to their favored ways of learning are less likely to become frustrated in class. Active, engaged learners have less time and motivation to create disturbances in the classroom.

Brain Research

God has created us with so much variety and placed us in a world we can explore. Thank God for the magnificence of creation, especially as seen in children under our care. God has made our brains marvelously ready to do the work of learning.

The past few years have seen an explosion in research about the brain and how it affects learning. New imaging techniques are making it possible to discover where in the brain certain activities take place. Research is also being done in critical and optimal times for learning. Some learning functions appear to be developed at a certain point. For example, some research suggests that if a child is born with certain vision problems and they are not treated early, the vision does not develop later—even if the physical problem is fixed. Other learning functions are easier at particular times in our development but not impossible at other times. For example, research indicates that it is easier to learn a second language before the the age of thirteen, but it is certainly possible to learn a second language after that age.

The more we find out about the human body, especially the brain, the more complex and marvelous we find it. We echo the words of Psalm 139:14: "I praise you, for I am fearfully and wonderfully made. Wonderful are your works; that I know very well."

Our very making is a miracle. Our first months are of tremendous importance, as a baby's brain is changing dramatically right after birth. The brain, which is still developing, is rapidly producing the connections that are the foundation of all future learning.

What Does This Mean for Teaching?

Nurturing and stress or trauma have different effects on a child's future interest in and readiness for learning. Stress can literally block learning. We cannot consider only what we want children to learn but must also think about environmental factors that affect learning. We need to know how to take advantage of the brain's natural bent toward learning.

The brain is always looking for patterns and meaning before storing knowledge long term. With any stimulus, the brain asks, "Does it make sense? Does it have meaning?" The answers depend on how a person feels about what just happened or how it relates to previous experience.

Furthermore, you cannot ignore biological needs without decreasing your effectiveness. Do not lecture, for instance, when the children have already used up their prime time for thinking. Think of learning as a balance of taking in and digesting. Adults can take in only about ten to twenty minutes of new information without needing to digest or process it in some way. We have to connect new input with things that already have meaning for us or to respond to new information in some way. When people focus for ten to eighteen minutes, they need about two to five minutes of down time to connect what they heard. If required to focus for fifty minutes, a person needs approximately thirty minutes before being ready to absorb more information. You will get more actual learning by stringing together several shorter teaching sessions.

The number of minutes a child can focus on any one thing is generally equal to the child's age plus two minutes. For example, a two-year-old can focus for about four minutes before needing to move or talk. An eleven-year-old can focus for about thirteen minutes maximum. Within one class, natural differences in development may mean some children focus several minutes less than others. A breath of fresh air, movement, or deep breathing can create a break that recharges and renews focus. People also perk up when you move from one type of activity to another.

Finally, take advantage of timing. People remember best the first and last thing said to them, so make it count. Instead of taking roll or chatting at the beginning of class, teach new material while the brain is fresh. Think of the two or three main points you want the children to remember. Structure short teaching segments around each point, and then review the main points right before closing. The next week, give the children an opportunity to practice skills or review information.

Practice, Practice

Think about all the things you have learned to do in your life. You probably have abilities and responses that are almost automatic. Practicing and simply visualizing behavior create a similar effect in many instances. That is why business leaders visualize themselves making a successful presentation and coaches say, "See yourself going over that bar."

Practice makes perfect. Well, not exactly. The more you practice and review a process, the easier it is to choose that process during a crisis or to remember it when needed. That is exactly why it is important to rehearse positive choices and correct information. If you do homework wrong over and over, you are going to learn the wrong way really well. If you rehearse a nonconfrontational way to respond if someone teases you, you might find yourself responding that way.

Practice makes not perfect but permanent. Why, then, do we often skip hands-on learning with children, reserving real work and ministry for when they grow up? Children are hungry for real-life experiences.

What do you remember from your own childhood? Do you remember words your Sunday school teacher spoke? play time with friends? real experiences? If you remember words, you probably have strong emotions attached to them, such as fear, shame, or exhilaration. Experiences are what we remember most.

In general, we remember only about five percent of what we hear, twenty percent of what we see and hear, fifty percent of what we discuss, but seventy-five percent of what we practice. When we teach others or use our learning immediately, we remember ninety percent. One way we can use our learning is to create a project or do something with it in real life. Help children learn hands-on to love their neighbors by raking leaves, making favors for people limited in their ability to leave home, or serving drinks at a volunteer breakfast. The practice of ministry helps teach what it means to be a disciple.

Another way children build experiences is by playing out what they just learned. Play is one way children process what happens to them. Therefore, teachers need to include time for children to play. However, children need play that is not predetermined by toys that are scripted by movies and advertising. They need to be free to imagine and to incorporate Bible stories and lesson themes into their play. It is easier to learn something new if you have previous related experience to connect the learning to. Both play and real-life activities create the experiential base that helps children connect to new learning.

Experiential activities and play are sometimes skipped in a lesson plan because of time constraints or because someone thinks they are not a wise use of the time. However, they are probably the most effective way to help children learn.

Implications for Peacemaking

To change behavior, we must start with changed thinking, as Romans 12:2 reminds us: "Be transformed by the renewing of your minds, so that you may discern what is the will of God—what is good and acceptable and perfect." Peace can be practiced until it is the brain's first choice.

If we care about peace, we also must take seriously the effect of stress and stimulation in all children's lives. If children live in perpetual fear of gunshots, there is little hope for their ability to remember what is taught in school. Memory gives way to fear and survival instincts. In contrast, children who are surrounded by caring adults have a better foundation for healthy emotional development, responsible choices, and solid relationships later in life. We truly cannot have peace without justice or peacemaking without nurturing all the children of our world.

Chapter Seven

Dealing With Feelings

"As God's chosen ones, holy and beloved, clothe yourselves with compassion, kindness, humility, meekness, and patience.... Forgive each other... And let the peace of Christ rule in your hearts" (Colossians 3:12-13, 15).

These words to the Colossians call us to let peace govern our actions. Even if compassion and patience are not part of our nature, we are to put on and practice them. Even if kindness, forgiveness, and love do not come naturally, we are to clothe ourselves with them and let peace rule in our lives. Emotions are directly related to peacemaking.

In fact, all experience is tied to emotion. When you sing the national anthem, for example, the meaning of the words is tied to feelings about your country and to other experiences of singing the anthem.

Can you remember when you learned to ride a bike? Is there a feeling attached to that experience? Do you remember the surprise you felt the first time you realized that your parent had let go and you were balancing on your own? You probably had that same feeling when you learned something else that initially seemed incomprehensible, such as solving algebra equations or playing an intricate piano piece.

When planning a lesson, it is easy to focus on information. We are not, however, pouring what we know into empty vessels. We teach the whole child, with all his or her experiences affecting the learning and with attitudes and emotions that must be factored in. Learning is meaning-driven and framed by emotion.

The emotional state affects whether a person retains or discards information and acts with reason or goes into survival mode. If you do not pay attention to emotions and feelings, you may be wasting your preparation for teaching. Jesus told us to love God with heart, soul, mind, and strength. Loving God—and learning faith—involves the whole child.

Emotional Intelligence

Emotional intelligence consists of the skills and abilities related to emotions and motivation. Almost everywhere that you find information about brain research and learning, you find discussion of skills or abilities associated with emotional intelligence.

In most expositions, emotional intelligence encompasses the ability to
- Identify and recognize your emotions
- Manage your emotions
- Motivate yourself
- Overcome frustrations and setbacks
- Empathize with others
- Enable and strengthen relationships with others
- Use people skills

Obviously, children are not born with fully developed emotional intelligence. It is a learning process, but it is important for the first steps to take place in early childhood.

Identifying and Recognizing Your Emotions—As we grow, we develop our awareness and attention to our own emotions. Adults, for instance, can often see frustration building in a toddler before the child knows he or she is upset. Mature individuals have learned that emotions affect actions, and they pay attention to their emotional state. Children learn emotional patterns as they observe adult reactions and listen to them talk about feelings.

Managing Your Emotions—The ability to manage one's emotions begins in the first few years of life. Most adults have learned to monitor how they react to emotions they feel. Adults may tell themselves, *I've had all I can take today. I need to be careful how I react in this meeting. I'm on edge, but it isn't fair to take it out on these people.* Such self-management starts in small ways as a child learns to control impulses and delay gratification. Immediate feedback is passed over for a larger, long-term reward. Controlling impulses, calming self, and reframing (looking at things in a new perspective) are all ways to manage emotions. Proverbs 29:8, 11 reminds us of the importance of managing emotion: "Scoffers set a city aflame, but the wise turn away wrath.… A fool gives full vent to anger, but the wise quietly holds it back." Anger itself is not wrong, but uncontrolled expression of anger can be foolish or destructive.

Managing emotions does not mean ignoring them. If emotions are not expressed or acknowledged, they can cause serious problems. If we do not work through grief, we can become stuck in depression. Unchecked fear can change to panic or anger. When anger is ignored, it may simmer into rage or turn into depression. Without expression, communication, or outlet, love can become jealousy or possessiveness, either of which can ruin a relationship. Emotions are a part of human life, and we can choose to act on them in positive ways. That is part of emotional intelligence.

Motivating Yourself and Overcoming Frustrations and Setbacks—A related area of emotional intelligence has to do with motivating yourself and overcoming frustration. Motivation depends heavily on the ability to delay gratification: focusing resources and ignoring distractions to achieve something in the future. Self-motivation primarily has to do with establishing and pursuing goals, as well as with persisting and coping with setbacks. Adults can guide children to set and meet goals and reframe situations so that they persist despite obstacles in their way.

Empathizing With Others—Emotional intelligence includes having empathy for others. Empathy means a person cares about others and, even more, connects with other people: understanding them, reading their body language, and imagining how they feel.

Enabling and Strengthening Relationships and Using People Skills—Finally, emotional intelligence includes the ability to develop relationships, which includes how to be a friend and how to interact with others. It also includes people skills, such as the ability to influence and persuade others, make someone feel at ease, and comfort another.

The Bible gives some insight on emotional intelligence:

- Ephesians 4:26: "Be angry but do not sin; do not let the sun go down on your anger."
- James 3:16-18: "For where there is envy and selfish ambition, there will also be disorder and wickedness of every kind. But the wisdom from above is first pure, then peaceable, gentle, willing to yield, full of mercy and good fruits, without a trace of partiality or hypocrisy. And a harvest of righteousness is sown in peace for those who make peace."

The Bible calls us to manage our emotions and motivate ourselves to act in peaceable, gentle ways. The promise is that we will receive a harvest well worth the effort. And that harvest includes peace.

Emotional Intelligence and Peace

It is obvious that we must work on emotional intelligence to help children with peacemaking. In particular, peacemaking skills rely on control of impulsivity, relationship skills, and the identification and management of feelings. Children need to work on curbing impulsivity so that they will not find themselves in one conflict after another. Relationship skills have to do with getting along with others, which is a major part of living in peace. Finally, being able to identify and manage emotions helps a person moderate anger or panic and respond peacefully.

How can you affect impulsivity? As children learn to plan responses rather than react, they have real chances to change impulsive habits when confronted with aggression or conflict. A rehearsed behavior is more likely to become the actual response, particularly during stressful moments. Help children plan and practice peaceful responses. Human beings can learn to respond in calm and practiced ways. Let the children know that we do not stop emotion but that we learn how to shape our behavior when we are aware of our feelings.

Another way you can help is by teaching children relationship skills. Upper elementary children, for whom peers are becoming increasingly important, desperately need to work on understanding, listening to, and communicating with peers. You can help them as you talk about situations and how characters in stories or plays could be better friends or more effectively influence others.

For all children, a primary peacemaking skill is naming and identifying feelings. Recognizing their own feelings helps them in overcoming impulsivity. Recognizing others' feelings gives them insight for problem solving. Children also need to learn that feelings change over time and that it is often advisable to let feelings cool before taking action.

Managing our emotions, motivating ourselves, and developing empathy and relationship skills are lifelong endeavors. Emotional intelligence is something you can work on, no matter what age level you teach.

Toddlers and Preschoolers

In *Identity: Youth and Crisis* (New York: W.W. Norton and Company, Inc., 1968), Erik Erikson discusses emotional development in terms of achieving healthy balances of trust, will, and other characteristics. His theories help us understand what developmental tasks people work on at different ages.

Erikson describes how children who are two and younger are working on a basic emotional balance of trust versus mistrust and will versus shame and doubt. They need consistent, calm caregivers who give them security and set reasonable boundaries. Toddlers and two-year-olds are naturally self-centered and prelogical. You cannot reason with them; however, you can help them develop empathy for others' feelings.

One way to develop empathy is by providing commentary as children exhibit feelings. In the gym Sally shoves Mike off the toy car. Mike screams. Their teacher rushes over. You note to your own class, "Uh-oh. Mike is angry. He and Sally both want the car. People shouldn't shove one another, because they could hurt someone. Sally is upset, too. Look, the teacher is rolling the car with both Sally and Mike on it. They can share it. They look happy."

Whenever you can, give toddlers and two-year-olds some words to use for their feelings. A child is trying over and over to get all the blocks to stay on the cart she is rolling. Either a bout of tears or a tantrum is near. You say, "You look frustrated. Would you like some help?"

Sometime in the preschool years, children begin to work on what Erikson calls initiative. This is the stage when children seem to thrust themselves on you with constant questions and by hurling their bodies toward yours, even when hugging. They are seeing what they can make happen. Familiarity and security enable them to feel confident enough to explore. They need to test out their ability to cause things, but they also need boundaries so that exercising their initiative will not endanger them.

Elementary Children

Elementary children need structure. They love rules and telling how things are supposed to be done. They also need to try out competencies in areas such as sports, music, youth organizations, choirs, and so forth. That is why Erikson calls this age a time of industry. Adults need to ensure that children do not feel too stretched or, on the other hand, unchallenged.

Children this age need to learn that we cannot change another person's feelings. Help them practice emotional skills related to others:

- Really listen to what other people are saying.
- Acknowledge what others are saying with comments such as "oh," "yes," and so forth.
- Name feelings that you observe: "It sounds to me like you are feeling nervous (or furious or excited)."

• When you cannot do anything, grant imaginary wishes: "You are so angry that your friend ate the last cookie. I wish I could open the oven door and pull out a whole pan just for you."

Teaching About Feelings

Drama and stories are two particularly useful ways to help children explore feelings. To help children learn to associate body language and expressions with emotions, you can let them play charades to guess which feelings are acted out. Someone is pacing and wringing hands: The person is worried or anxious. The children learn the names for emotions and how to recognize those feelings by nonverbal cues.

Stories are also valuable teaching tools to use to talk about feelings. Children do not analyze their own behavior as easily as they comment on that of a character or puppet. For instance, if you read *Alexander and the Terrible, Horrible, No Good, Very Bad Day,* by Judith Viorst, you can ask, "How did Alexander feel when he had a cavity? Look at this picture. How does he feel here?" Book illustrations express feelings that you can use for discussion with preschool and elementary children.

You do not have to spend weeks on lessons about emotions. As you tell stories, ask questions: "In this picture, how does it look like Jacob feels?" Encourage the children to identify body language and expressions in the stories. Whenever you can, point out body language and expression of emotion in videos, dramas, or other media.

Give the students opportunities to name the emotions they feel: "How are you feeling today?"

Teach the children ways to manage anger. Ask for ways people react when they are angry at school, at home, at church, at a ball game, or at Scouts. List the various reactions they tell you. Discuss the consequences of each reaction. Ask the children to name ways to get rid of bottled up feelings of anger without hurting anyone. They may name pounding a pillow, exercising, yelling, crying, throwing away a symbol of what makes them angry or writing it on paper and tearing the paper into bits. Also suggest that they talk to someone, jump or run in place, or play with a calming media (such as modeling dough or water).

Work on delayed gratification by having some plan that requires saving up for a reward. For example, "If everyone behaves for four weeks, we will have a party." Or, "If everyone brings a Bible for two weeks in a row, the next week I will bring a treat." Encourage them to have patience to wait for God's plan. Let them know that God's plan is so often far better than any we could imagine. If you can, give an example from your own life.

Try It Out

Here are some activities to help the children deal with feelings.

Burdens Race (elementary)

Materials: books or other heavy objects that can be safely carried

Directions: Play this game to illustrate how anger affects us. Divide the class into two groups to play a relay game. Mark a start line and a finish line. Have each runner carry heavy books or other objects as they run to the finish line and back. They then pass the books to the next runner. After the teams have run the race, ask, "Could you have run faster without the weights?" Talk about the burden of carrying anger with us. Give everyone a chance to pantomime throwing his or her anger in a wastebasket.

Include these teachings:

- We are not bad just because we are angry.
- We can decide how we are going to act and can express anger in ways that don't hurt anyone.
- Any time a person chooses to work out feelings and differences in a nonviolent way, the person is helping to make peace.

Write It Down (elementary)

Materials: paper, pencils

Directions: Give children a chance to write down what they do when they experience emotions. (For younger children, use the sentences as a discussion exercise rather than a writing one.)

- When I feel sad, I...
- One thing that helps me when I'm sad is...
- When I'm happy, I love to...
- I feel brave when...
- I worry about...
- I am afraid when...
- I feel important when...
- I get angry when...
- When I'm angry, I usually...
- When someone teases me, I...

- I am proud that I can...
- I have the power to...
- I'm learning to stay out of trouble when I'm angry. Instead, I...
- I can talk things over with...

Point out that although feelings are always okay, people must react appropriately.

Matching Feelings (younger elementary)

Materials: index cards with a feeling written on each card (happy, glad, angry, sad, and so forth), pictures from magazines that match the feelings listed

Directions: Let the children match the pictures with the cards that describe the emotions pictured.

Feelings Badge (elementary)

Materials: nametags, felt-tip markers

Directions: Let each child decorate a nametag with words or illustrations of how he or she feels at the moment: excited, scared, happy, joyful, tired, uncertain, and so forth. They should wear it as a badge for the day. Ask those who are willing to tell why they chose a particular feeling. Make the badges more than once. Each time point out these things:
- Our names remain the same week to week, but our feelings change.
- We are not the same as our feelings.
- We can shape our actions despite our feelings.

Feelings Thermometer (younger elementary)

Materials: posterboard, felt-tip markers, button, string

Directions: Draw a large thermometer on a piece of posterboard. Instead of numbers, write feelings on the gauge (see the feelings chart on page 37). Thread a button on a string. Drape the string on the poster over the thermometer, and tape it at the top and bottom. Ask the children to move the button to mark feelings they have at given times.

Feelings Game (elementary)

Materials: ball or beanbag

Directions: Explain that sometimes recognizing an emotion helps us manage it when we experience it again. Pass a ball around a circle of players. Turn away for a few seconds and then say, "Stop!" Whoever has the ball when you turn back answers a question, such as, "When did you feel excited?" or, "When were you anxious?" Players start the ball going around again when you turn away and say, "Go!" This game gives a chance to connect new vocabulary with their experiences. Later, talk about ways to change feelings by exercising, by talking to someone when you are sad, or by taking ten deep breaths when you are upset.

Thumbs Up (younger elementary)

Directions: Have the children put their thumbs up for yes or thumbs down for no to each statement as you read it:

- When I'm happy, I sing.
- When I'm angry, I take deep breaths.
- When I'm excited, I jump around.
- When I'm joyful, I smile.
- When I'm sad, I cry.
- When I'm frustrated, I stomp my feet.
- When I'm sad, I tell someone.
- When I'm angry, I yell.
- When I'm furious, I hit something.
- When I'm frustrated, I cry.

Tell the children that our feelings just happen, but we can choose how to act. Some people hit or kick others or otherwise hurt them when they are angry, but a better way to handle anger would be to take deep breaths, get some exercise, or punch a pillow. Ask, "What would help us when we are sad?" (tell someone, exercise, watch a funny show, do something with friends)

Chapter Eight

Peace in the Nursery

Peace-based learning begins in the nursery. Parents, other caregivers, and preschool teachers are laying the foundation for future peacemaking. Peace skills depend heavily on emotional intelligence, which has its sensitive period in early childhood. Language skills, which are crucial for talking about differences and solutions, are related to a child's exposure to human relationships, stories, and talking. The first three years are when children lay down critical connections for learning, including peace skills. Peacemaking begins with how we treat children in the nursery.

It takes a special person to work with toddlers and two-year-olds. The teacher's attitude makes a difference. What message does a caregiver send when he or she looks frazzled and has jangled nerves from the children's constant crying or whining? when he or she is relaxed, and the children are content and interested? Toddlers and two-year-olds do need special teachers, people who can help them navigate in a brand-new world. When they can stem the tide of rising wails, calm the children, and create security, proficient teachers end up with a more peaceful day not just for the children but for themselves.

Setting Up the Room

Start by examining where you teach. Does foot traffic disrupt a perfect spot for quiet play? Get down to see what the room looks like at the child's level. Does it seem exciting or scary? reassuring or overwhelming?

Make the space interesting but safe. Allow exploration while eliminating danger. Make sure the toys match the children's abilities so that they will not become bored or frustrated. Store toys in the same places so that children can find them and help put them away. Have some familiar toys to provide security, but include some challenging ones as well. Common household items, such as pots and pans or containers, provide comfortable security.

Be aware that you are teaching through your room. Toys and activities that encourage interaction, such as large-motor toys that fit more than one, encourage toddlers to play by each other's side. A basin of water and several dipping cups will also encourage interaction.

You also need a cool-down spot, a quiet space where children can spend time when they need to get control of themselves. Arrange your classroom with spaces for individual time: an overstuffed chair, a box with cushions, or a cozy corner. Toddlers need a place to withdraw sometimes. Infants and toddlers may want to lie on a pillow and watch from a safe distance. Do not use this spot for punishment or time-out, or it will no longer feel like a safe place.

Create a comfort zone. Display pictures of the children and, if possible, of their families. Be sure that purchased posters and pictures include a variety of ethnic groups. You will want to include all the groups represented in your church.

Have some open floor space, and plan places where children can enjoy sensory experiences: fingerpainting, modeling dough, water play, and touching textures.

Teach Through Your Own Behavior

You are laying a template for the children's future relationships. Think about your example. To increase peace and calm in the nursery, act as you want the children to act: Be polite and respectful. Show them how to play in the home area together or how to take turns on the slide. They do not automatically know how. Give them choices, and respect and remember the challenges they face.

They love to say, "No!" so give them chances to do so. You can do this by asking silly questions: "Do we wear hats on our feet? No! Do we eat books? No!" Offer choices, but not when you cannot accept one of the choices. Do not ask, "Do you want to go with us?"—the other choice is "No!" Give power to the toddlers by letting them choose between two activities you approve: "Do you want to watch the movie or sit quietly with a book while others watch?" In a world where they have little authority, the power to choose is healing.

Healing and peace also come as you respect individuality. Not every child has to react the same. Let children warm up to an activity. Some may get involved immediately, while others need time to watch first. Do not push. Think how new the entire world is to the nursery children. Use language, too, to let them know how important they are: "God made you special. We like the way you love singing." Or, "Ahmad has such a friendly smile. That is a gift from God."

Remember three major challenges nursery children face. First, they have learning limits. Second, their abilities do not always measure up to what they want to do, so they get frustrated. Third, they do not have all the language they need to communicate. Be alert for a child whose frustration is building. You may notice a child getting more tense, getting red in the face, stomping feet, treating toys rougher, or even vocalizing frustration. If you can meet the child's need or help him or her solve the problem, you may avert such aggressive acts as biting or tantrums.

Things to Remember

Keep the children interested. Plan lessons that have hands-on activities and a balance of predictability and surprises.

Be respectful when you talk to young children. First, do not talk about their behavior to another adult as if they are not there. That depersonalizes them. Next, when you need to get their attention, speak in a normal tone instead of yelling across the room. This may require getting up and going to where children are, but it is how you would treat an adult. Also, remember to talk to a child with respect when you check or change diapers.

Most of all, be aware that toddlers and two-year-olds have immediate reactions, as they have not yet learned control. Accept them for who they are, and you will eliminate your own stress and some of theirs.

When they misbehave, be firm, fair, and matter-of-fact. State what you expect them to do. Enforce without emotion any consequences to rules. Toddlers are often scared when they feel out of control. When you are calm, it helps them calm down.

Teach Through Their Behavior

First, the best way to encourage appropriate behavior is to acknowledge it when it occurs naturally. Catch them interacting peacefully and say, "I like the way Cammy and Lisa are working together on a puzzle" or, "Everyone is waiting for a turn. I am so proud."

Second, give the children time before you intervene in an argument (of course, not if safety is an issue). Getting along takes practice, so let them work at it. Wait a while to see if they will work out their differences. They may choose to negotiate turns in the play car or discover that there is room for two. They may compromise, which is excellent experience. Praise them for their cooperation.

Third, describe and label what you see. That is one way they learn what it means to be helpful or kind or frustrated. Do not rate children by saying "good girl" or "good boy." It is hard to live up to being good all the time, but a person can be proud to be helpful or kind and strive to be so again. Be sure to comment on behavior only: "Annie picked up all the blocks. I'm so proud" or, "Tyler made a picture for our new friend, Michelle. That's what I call thoughtful."

Whenever infants and toddlers interact in peaceful ways, comment on it and give the action a label: "You are playing together with the blocks. That's cooperation." If they are about to kick, throw, or hurt another child, and obviously decide not to, praise their good decision.

If you see them getting frustrated or angry, give them ways to express the emotion: "If you are angry, say, 'I'm angry!' It even helps to stomp your foot."

Tools to Use

Put these three techniques in your toolbelt for peace: let children be helpers, encourage listening, use books to teach peacemaking. First, you can provide opportunities for children as young as toddlers to be helpers. Toddlers can hand out napkins, pass out notes, or put the attendance slip on the door. All these jobs create pride. It is especially important for peacemaking when you can help them help others. Their help might be comforting a friend, helping to carry something, or joining another toddler in a search for a lost box of crayons. Emotional intelligence includes having empathy for others, and the seeds can be sown in the first two years.

Encourage listening. Toddlers need the same skills as other children in order to solve problems. You can begin to work on basic listening skills.

Point out sounds around you: the crunchy sound when they eat carrots, footsteps passing by, a far-off phone ringing, the sound a zipper makes when it is pulled, or snaps clicking shut.

Play different kinds of music for them to listen to. Move to music. Let them repeat sounds after you as you read a story: "Who-ooo-sh went the wind."

Use books to start conversations. Find stories where the characters are helpful and are learning friendship skills or practicing them. Make books about the children in your class. Feature their helpful acts or the skills they have: "Carole can jump and run."

Language skills are critical for future problem solving.

Security and Self-esteem

One of the first peace steps is that of accepting and caring about yourself. Start peace education by building the children's self-esteem whenever you can. One way to build self-esteem with an infant is to reflect back his or her expressions, which affirms the child as an individual. You also build children up when you let them be the helper and give them choices, such as what to play or which bib to wear.

Routines and familiar procedures build self-esteem, as they help a child feel secure and in control. Our brains are always looking for pattern and routine, but young children need familiarity to feel safe. A child who receives predictable, caring responses feels better about self than one who is treated unpredictably and with anger.

Another self-esteem booster is when you protect their space. Let them know that their possessions are safe and that you will not tolerate aggression toward their person. This eliminates a sense of threat and may help avoid some aggressive behaviors. (Biting, for instance, is sometimes motivated by being scared or overwhelmed.)

Meet their physical needs, such as diaper changes, snacks, and rest. Also give physical reassurance, such as hugs and cuddles. Younger children, particularly, need physical touch (in appropriate ways, of course). With infants and toddlers, whether or not they receive touch and comforting affects their ability to bond and interact with others. Policies that restrict touching children do not usually include the nursery, but check your church's policies for recommended safeguards.

This is a good place to mention that you should always have at least two adults for every group of children, no matter how small the group.

One person should not be assigned to work alone with children, as having two adults helps protect the children from abuse and the teacher from unfounded accusations.

Map Out Your Plan

For a more peaceful classroom, be aware of and respond to your own tension. It will relay through the group if you do not deal with it first. Your tension increases their tension, so do not let your stress build up. If it has been a hard day, do some relaxation exercises and try to get some perspective on the day. If you are upset, be sure you calm down before you act. The children are learning how to behave by watching you.

Always keep in mind the child's perspective. Infants and toddlers are egocentric, thinking everything revolves around them. This means you do not need to take their reactions personally. If they will not let you pick them up or will not cooperate, it is not about you. Remember also that they cannot see another person's point of view unless you explain it (and maybe not then).

Try to phrase requests positively. As mentioned earlier, try to eliminate opportunities for them to say no, which can set up a battle of wills. A toddler usually wins such a battle, or makes the victory costly. Do not say, "Do you want to go to the gym now?" if you are definitely taking the class there. Say, "We are going to the gym. Do you want to march or walk?"

Examine your teaching plan for the proper amount of stimulation. Too much stimulation can make a child stressed or withdrawn.

Frequently Asked Questions

The following questions and responses may help you with common situations that occur in groups of infants, toddlers, and two-year-olds.

What if you notice a child who is alone in the corner and acting uninterested in play and withdrawn?

Try to find out what feeling is motivating the child. Did the child withdraw because she needed time alone, or does she feel scared or over-stimulated? Is she new to the group? Has something happened in her family, such as a new sibling or a move? Ask if the child wants a comfortable lap to sit in, and offer to read a story or to sort shapes.

If the child just wants to be left alone, make sure you can adequately supervise the child while letting her have her own space. Continue to check in on the child. Sometimes the child just needs time. Sometimes the child wants to be alone because she does not feel well. Look for flushed cheeks or a fever, which indicate that an illness is coming on.

What if a child throws a tantrum?

Remember that tantrums are part of a normal day. A toddler's emotional task is to develop will, to know what he or she can and cannot control. Toddlers experience much frustration over their limited ability and language, so tantrums are bound to happen. When a child has a tantrum, do the following:

- Keep the child safe.
- Let the child know you are there. Children may be scared by their own lack of control.
- Acknowledge his or her feelings. Suggest ways to express frustration.
- Assure the child that you accept him or her, even when the child has been out of control.
- Try to find out what feeling is motivating an action. Did the child withdraw because she needed time alone, or is she scared or overstimulated? Evaluate if your routine contributed by putting off lunch or nap time too long so that the child was hungry or tired. Is variety needed, including time to play outdoors? Was the tantrum caused by being angry and not having any words to describe the feeling?

What do I do when children fight over a toy?

Again, remind yourself that toddlers and two-year-olds are who they are. They do not yet see another person's perspective and really do not know how to share. At best, they engage in parallel play. Help them learn to interact peacefully when having to share toys.

Experienced teachers recommend four techniques: distraction, timers, turns, and trades. Distraction is just offering another toy or activity when a child wants what another has. Many teachers also use timers or hourglasses so that the children can see a visible marker for turns. Say, "When all the sand is in the bottom, it will be your turn with the truck. We will turn the hourglass over; when the sand runs out again, it will be someone else's turn."

Of course, timers rely on taking turns. Particularly with popular toys, get in the habit of emphasizing that each child can play a while, but that others will have a turn later. Monitor the children to make sure the turns happen. (Veteran teachers add, "Get multiples of popular toys, and have plenty of the same thing.")

Trading is a more complicated skill. Teach children to trade one desirable toy for another. Pick one out yourself, or say to the child, "Let's see if Sammy will trade a toy with you. What do you think Sammy might be willing to play with instead—the cookie cutters and modeling dough or the singing machine?" A young toddler may choose the toy you were going to trade. That is fine, for it is a distraction.

Often, two-year-olds can share a toy, if you participate in the play: "Tanisha, can you put a red one in? Matthew, find a yellow one. Tanisha's got another yellow one. Tanisha, put it in and then Matthew gets a turn."

When children are struggling to get control of a toy, use the situation to help them. Name the feelings you observe, and encourage appropriate behavior. Acknowledge the feelings of all children when more than one are involved: "Sydney, that hurt when you got pushed. Elise, I think you're feeling angry because you can't get the puzzle pieces to fit."

Describe what happened and remind them of appropriate behavior: "I saw Elise playing with the puzzle and having a hard time with the pieces. When Sydney tried to help her put a piece in, Elise pushed her down. We don't push people. You can use your words and say, 'I don't want help.'" Whenever possible, show children an appropriate behavior.

Help the toddlers solve the problem: "Elise, you could work the puzzle with Sydney, and you could each take a turn. Sydney, you could wait until Elise is through and have a turn then. Which will be okay with both of you?" As toddlers grow and become preschoolers, you can even ask them to suggest solutions.

Peace? Some Days, Yes!

Your description of other children's feelings, the work on listening skills, your own calm approach, and your peace education do all add up. Some days you will be frazzled, no doubt; however, your class can grow into peace skills for faithful living.

Chapter Nine

Growing as Peacemakers

Through your own inner peace, by setting the stage for learning, and by matching activities to children's development and learning preferences, discipline is less of a problem.

Just because children are behaving does not necessarily mean the classroom is a place of peace. Peace is wholeness and right relationships with God and neighbor. How do children learn peacemaking? How do we help children develop values and morals that reflect Christ's commandment to love God and neighbor? How do we help children to move from self-interest to decisions based on biblical, faith-centered principles?

Moral Decision Making

Moral decision making is a process that is influenced by a child's experiences and developmental stage.

Toddlers may not choose the right behavior if it seems in their interest to do otherwise. For instance, the cookie jar is not safe from a two-year-old if it is not out of reach or is not supervised. Since a toddler is not yet able to understand another person's perspective, you cannot really talk about whether the toddler's decisions are moral or not. The toddler's self-interest is basically biological.

Adult guidance is necessary. But it is difficult in the early years because two- and three-year-olds are unable to compromise, and they see only their own needs. Reasoning is not useful at all, because they are not logical thinkers. Any motivation to do right must emphasize the emotions. For instance, an adult can show that he or she is happy when a toddler helps others. Caregivers can also teach compassion by giving insight into how others feel.

When a child is between the ages of four and six, both parents and teachers should begin teaching morals as rules: "We tell the truth here." Being exposed to general principles for decision making may help children recognize that there is a system for choosing behavior.

Children also learn morality as they experience the consequences of their actions, coupled with adult explanation. Children will not enjoy it when adults allow them to experience the negative consequences of their actions. But as long as the child will not be endangered, that is okay. Who would enjoy being grounded or losing an allowance? It is important for adults to let children express their feelings about discipline.

Natural consequences, such as the following, help teach the concept of cause and effect:

• If you throw the cereal on the floor in a rage, you will not be given more cereal until tomorrow.

• If you break the cookie jar when you weren't supposed to touch it, you will not be given more cookies until you have saved up and bought a new jar.

• If you take your birthday money to school against parental advice and school policy and then lose it, your money will not be replaced.

When children are school age, decision making (including the choice of right or wrong) is linked to a child's sense of competence. As children first begin to understand the wideness of the world around them, they need to have their own abilities confirmed, not just in achievements but also in doing right. Adults need to help children view their efforts as successful. Honest feedback, however, is important: "I liked the way you tried to include Sam in the game. I bet next time you will get it to work. You learned something, didn't you?"

School-age children also need rules and explanations about what is acceptable: "In our time together, we will not comment on other people's appearance. People's feelings might get hurt."

Another part of morality is caring about others. Elementary children are old enough to learn caring firsthand. We all learn much of our faith from service to others because we find God at work there already. Let children learn the rewards of helping others.

Children are receptive to learning about what is right and wrong. An adult's role is to enforce consequences, demonstrate positive attitudes toward authority, and make sure children know it is okay to talk about faith and problems. Both parents and teachers need to establish habits of communication. Moral decision making depends on continued conversations, especially about how to live as people of faith.

Faithful Living

To talk about living out our faith, we need to understand how faith develops. Even when children are not old enough to profess faith, faith is still present. Young children have an experienced faith. God is with them, through the church and also through intuitive experiences. They live in an atmosphere of faith as others tell them the stories, nurture them, and design ways for them to be a part of the worshiping church.

Elementary children have a faith in action. They are a part of the church through choirs, clubs, and classes. They want to belong. They are trying out all their competencies in various avenues of service: acolytes, choir members, puppeteers, and so forth.

Youth need to be allowed to question in order to move to a faith that is truly theirs. Their development, both the emotional task of forming identity and their new cognitive ability to explore abstract ideas, makes youth a natural time to ask, "Is the faith that my parents gave me true? Of all I've been taught, what do I believe?"

Those adults who have moved through questioning have a faith that has become their own. If adults are allowed to search out answers so that their belief system becomes personally applied, they come to a faith that they accept and make a basis for living. They usually have begun answering some basic questions:

- Can I trust God?
- How do I know how to act?
- Can I do what I want?
- What about God's will?
- For what purpose was I created?
- What gifts has God given me for life and ministry?

The answers to these questions grow out of emotional tasks in childhood, those of developing a sense of trust and competence, of determining what one has the ability and freedom to do. In light of God's work in our lives, our interactions with others, and our emotional development, we apply Scripture to our experience and form working answers to guide us.

Showing the Way

Psalm 119:105 sums it up: "Your word is a lamp to my feet and a light to my path." Part of your role as a teacher is to explain and apply Scriptures to help the children live out their faith. First, you demonstrate how you live out your faith. You tell them how your own faith shapes your actions. Explain why you come to church and why you participate in worship. Let children know about your own habits of prayer, Bible reading, and mission work. You also share your faith through teachable moments: "This passage makes me think of how we felt when Lila moved away. I realized that I needed to trust that God will take care of us." Put your spontaneous prayers into words.

Besides telling about your faith, find ways to recognize how the children are growing up in the faith. You want them to know that you expect them to grow in discipleship. Highlight and recognize occasions such as these that show progress on the Christian journey:

- Getting a Bible when they are old enough to read
- Being old enough to attend children's choir
- Putting faith in action (joining the peer mediators at school, doing service projects, and so forth)

Help the children find religious meaning in daily experience. At one church, a youth minister and his son were looking at how light was shining through fabric and making patterns on the floor. "That would make a good sermon, wouldn't it, Daddy," the son said. He had absorbed the lesson: God is all around us, and everything can communicate God's truth. Faith is caught as children are exposed to it. Peacemaking is also.

Skills That Help Children Live Peacefully

Consider Colossians 3:15: "And let the peace of Christ rule in your hearts, to which indeed you were called in the one body." Peacemaking is something to which we are called, one aspect of faithful living.

You can teach some skills that children need for peacemaking. They need a vocabulary for talking about emotions, the ability to brainstorm and choose solutions, and the ability to listen. These skills might be called prerequisites for peacemaking. In Matthew 18:15-20, when Jesus is talking about solving conflict among church members, the word *listen* appears four times. Listening is a critical skill for problem solving.

Two other peacemaking basics are accepting and appreciating self, and accepting and celebrating differences in others.

Both Sunday and weekday teachers already work on these skills, with lessons on self-esteem, family, community, and appreciating our differences. But what value is a tool you do not know you have? When headlines and news bulletins make the world's conflicts known, children may wonder if there is hope for the future. The unknown causes fear, and we are often anxious and afraid when we have no influence. You can help children by letting them know some steps for peace and how to use them (see "Peacemaking Basics" below). You can also help by giving the children chances to work on their own conflicts and interpersonal problems. Adults sometimes think that because children are small, their problems are small. Being left out at recess or being caught between two feuding friends may seem minor, but they are important to the people involved. These situations need peacemaking.

To avoid some interpersonal problems and to give children guidance for such situations, do problem solving about common incidents in the classroom, such as shoving in line or grabbing the best supplies. When you ignore such issues, it belies your commitment to peacemaking. Discussing issues may yield creative solutions from the children.

Peacemaking Basics
Infants and Toddlers

Peace education for our youngest children focuses on the self. Infants and toddlers are naturally egocentric, so they are not ready for conflict resolution. They need help making peace with themselves. As parents and caregivers help infants and toddlers negotiate frustration and feel loved and important, they lay the foundations for peace.

Next come the two- and three-year-olds. Few two-year-olds are at peace with the world. Don't we know it? Two- and three-year-olds are learning what they can make happen by exercising their will. A gap often exists between what they want to do and what they are able to do, so they frequently experience frustration. When teachers help their students cope with frustration and avoid aggression, they are working on peace. When caregivers show children how to defer gratification for a greater reward, they teach peace. Two- and three-year-olds also work on peace as they learn how others feel. As they learn about themselves and their own emotions, their developing vocabulary prepares them for later problem solving.

Of course, some problem solving goes on even at this stage. Two- and three-year-olds are moving from parallel play to more truly interactive social play. As they play, sharing toys and expressing feelings with appropriate actions are daily challenges and peacemaking tasks. Using words instead of hitting becomes a guideline for future peacemaking. Most importantly, the attitudes and actions of parents and caregivers provide a pattern for the children's interactions.

Preschool Through Early Elementary

Peace steps grow as children grow. Three- to five-year-olds are learning how to get along. Later, they learn ways to cope with anger, conflict, and the breach of boundaries in their group. They continue to work on expressing emotions and listening, as well as valuing themselves and others.

As children develop a sense of "my class," whether it is a school class, a play group, or Sunday school, they begin to experience the lack of peace in the group. Teachers have ample opportunities to teach problem solving and to model win/win approaches. Developing a plan for peace appeals to initiative-seeking four- to six-year-olds, as long as they are working on a concrete situation. Bring to circle time issues such as pushing in line, monopolizing toys, and so forth.

In early elementary years, children still need help identifying and expressing feelings. Let them use puppets to act out scenarios. This is particularly useful, since they do not easily analyze their own behavior or verbalize emotions and concerns. Impromptu puppet skits give them an outlet for emotions. Through books they can also examine problems they do not know how to verbalize.

Preschool through early elementary grades are prime years for work on listening through discussion, rhymes, guessing games, and directed questions. Listening practice will help them when they try to hear someone else's viewpoint during future problem solving.

An important part of peace education at any level is accepting and valuing self. You build peace when you build self-esteem, because how children feel about themselves shapes their interactions with others and can block or enhance learning. You can work on peace skills with any activity on self-esteem, such as talking about hobbies, making collages about interests, or playing games to name one another's talents.

It is important, however, to remember that preschoolers and early elementary children are not yet logical thinkers. Parents and teachers can elicit ideas from the children and teach them routines for getting along, but pulling it all together is still the adult's role.

Middle Elementary

School-age children are aware of the need for peace in the community, state, and beyond. They know about violence and conflict in their own classes and in the school and community. They may be concerned about peace in the state and country, or even in the world.

If children feel helpless about an event that is beyond their control, help them brainstorm ways to do something (send cards to children in Afghanistan, pray for peace, and so forth). You can also avert a sense of helplessness by teaching them some steps for peacemaking.

Peace Steps

Step 1: Have peace in yourself. Understand that God made you special. Care about yourself.

Step 2: Be able to name your feelings. Try to understand other people's feelings.

Step 3: Accept and care about others. Celebrate human diversity.

Step 4: Make peace with friends and family. Learn to use conflict resolution. Learn to be a friend.

Middle-elementary children also begin to develop a sense of history, which helps in understanding timelines and cause and effect. Since this age group is ready to try out new interests and activities, sponsor peace camps and clubs. Capitalize on their desire to belong. Let them apprentice in problem solving, peer mediation, and conflict resolution. Help them work on identifying and managing emotions.

School-age children can also try problem solving, since they can reason in specific situations. However, they will still not generalize from one situation to a universal rule or easily analyze their own behavior and feelings. The more situations they can examine and roleplay, the better, as they are then more likely to apply the learning in a similar situation. Teach them that there is not just one way to respond but many options in any circumstance. Teach them the following:

- God can help us change.
- God will help us act in peace.
- God reconciled the world through Christ and has entrusted us with the work of reconciliation (2 Corinthians 5:18).

Preadolescent

Preadolescents are similar to other school-agers in readiness for peacemaking, except that the physical changes of puberty make acceptance of self and others a focal concern. Among preadolescent children, there is a great difference in physical development, as well as differing ability to understand abstract concepts. They are concerned with appearing different. They also tend to judge others quickly. Help them to be less judgmental and to develop empathy. Model an appreciation of diversity over exclusion of those who are different.

Preadolescents, like others, need to build up self-esteem. They need to feel unique and identify their gifts and talents. You can teach them how to affirm one another and themselves. Peace with self is, after all, the first steppingstone on the way to peace.

Friendship skills are important. Friendships are often where hurt feelings and conflicts begin. Talk with children about not jumping to conclusions, not gossiping, and being honest about how they feel. Help them learn to listen to a friend and to stand by each other when others ridicule. Encourage them to make their group a no-ridicule zone.

Give preadolescents some help with their own situations. Let them anonymously list problems they encounter. Read the problems out loud, and have the group suggest various responses. Also give tips on handling anger: cool down before discussing something, release anger in safe ways, calm down through relaxation or exercise. Invite a counselor to talk about when to ignore bullying and name-calling and when and how to ask that others treat you respectfully.

Teach safety. Preteens, as well as younger children, need to know what to do if someone picks up a gun, even in play. Gun safety instructors say, "Don't try to persuade someone not to shoot. Don't ever assume a gun is not loaded. Get out of the area; then call for help." Since preteens often are beginning to participate in activities without parents, they may also run into situations where drugs or alcohol are being used. Teach them that they can say, "I don't do that," and that they can call a parent or other adult to come get them.

Bridge the Differences

Do children and peacemaking go together? One Sunday the after-school group sang in worship and visited Sunday school. On that day, the Sunday school class was studying peace. What an irony. The group had oil-and-water division between "us" and "them." The discussion was not working because there was not any trust level. I asked each person to find a partner whom they did not know. I said, "Tell your partner about a friend who is different than you but still special." Suddenly the room was transformed. Voices got higher and louder with excitement. When I called a halt, I said, "Did you hear that? You had so much energy. You really like your friends, don't you? They're important to you, even though they're different. It is not just okay to be different from one another, but it is also energizing and fun. Tell me some of what you said." It worked. Children can bridge differences between "us" and "them," especially when you begin in concrete ways.

Try It Out

The following activities will help children develop peacemaking skills.

Talk About Situations (elementary)

Directions: This activity will help children develop empathy. Read aloud each situation below and then ask, "How do they feel? How could they tell someone how they feel?"

- Aimee found out that her friends Rebecca and Ashley made the soccer team and she didn't.
- Leann and Sophia won't talk to each other because each one thinks the other is angry about a recess game.
- Rachel wants to be one of the junior volunteers at the animal shelter. Melinda has one of two possible positions but keeps finding reasons not to go. Rachel doesn't know how to approach Melinda or the shelter about taking over the job.
- Carl wants to go to church to sing with the Joyful Sound choir. It is his dad's weekend, and his dad doesn't go to that church.
- Reid's older brother picks on him while walking home from school and even makes him stay outside once they get home.
- Matt's friend Elizabeth gets every video game she ever wants, but Matt has to save up for his. Recently, Elizabeth bought the last copy of the one Matt wanted.

Talk About How to Live in Peace (grades 2 through 6)

Directions: Discuss what each person could do in the following situations. Name four or five possible responses and what the consequences of each response would be.

- People always pick on me and push me around. What should I do?
- My brother and I always fight over staying out of each other's rooms.

- A girl is trying to break up a friendship between another girl and me.
- Someone is bullying me, and nothing works.
- I have this friend who is a crybaby and always tells on me.
- I know a girl whose parents got divorced. She thinks something is wrong because she doesn't feel like she loves her mom anymore.
- A guy in the neighborhood keeps asking me to smoke marijuana with him.
- Someone at school keeps getting in fights. He has a knife, but no one else knows.
- Everyone makes fun of me. Sometimes I want to give up.

In the situation where the friend is a crybaby and tells, you could
- Ignore it.
- Talk to the friend about how you feel.
- Ask advice from an adult.
- Tell the friend that you are not going to put up with it anymore, and the next time it happens quit playing with the friend until there is a change.

In the case of the person who fights and has a knife, it is a safety issue. You should
- Walk away from the danger.
- Tell an adult who can do something.
- Pray that no one gets hurt.

In the situation where the child fights with the brother about staying out of each other's rooms, you could
- Talk to the brother about how you feel.
- Work out times to be together and to be alone in your rooms.
- Ask a parent to intervene.
- Work out rules for being in each other's rooms.
- Tell the brother you want to make peace and ask for his help.
- Walk away any time there is a fight.

Daydream About Peace (grades 2 through 6)

Materials: newspaper to cover tables; felt, muslin, or sheets; permanent markers, special fabric crayons, or paint and brushes

Directions: Have the children do some deep breathing to relax. Then ask, "If you dreamed of a world where there was peace, what are some things you'd see in that world?" After the children respond, tell them to choose one dream to paint or draw on a cloth. Use the cloth in worship.

Learn Peace Steps (elementary)

Materials: paper and pencils

Directions: Review these steps until the children know them. Play games such as hangman or crossword puzzles to get familiar with the words in the steps. Have older children act out each one for others to guess.

Peacemaker Steps

A peacemaker

- Understands that he or she is a wonderful creation by God.
- Spends time with God to gain a sense of peace inside.
- Has feelings but tries to express them in nonhurtful ways.
- Names what is good about others and accepts them as they are.
- Practices kindness toward others.
- Tries not to hurt others.
- Celebrates human diversity.
- Tries to come up with nonviolent solutions when there is a conflict.
- Forgives others and asks for forgiveness when he or she has done wrong.

Chapter Ten

Practicing Peace

The more a behavior is practiced, or even visualized, the more likely the brain is to choose it in responding to a stimulus. Rehearsal does impact future performance. Practicing peace should therefore have an impact on children's behavior.

The challenge with children is that they understand only tangible examples and things they see, hear, and experience. That is why we call them concrete thinkers. We also mean that they do not generalize from specific examples to attain a basic concept. Children are still learning cause and effect, sequencing, and chronology. They are less able than youth or adults to analyze themselves and their behavior. These characteristics make them less likely to apply learning from one situation to another. A child can learn a peaceful response for one situation and not apply it to another.

The more case studies you can talk about and act out in peaceful ways, the more you help them learn peaceable responses to problems. You can help them practice peace.

Set It Up

Your first step is to set up your classroom for peacemaking. Give peacemaking some prestige. Have a peacemaker award or a bulletin board to acknowledge when children have acted with respect or have worked out differences.

Make space for peace. Have a cool-down spot that is not the same space used for time-out. Those who need to do problem solving need privacy. If other classmates can observe them, problem solvers cannot concentrate on reaching an agreement. Setting aside a space for conflict resolution also shows that it is important to learn to live in peace.

Stock your peace space with an item to designate whose turn it is to talk. The item can be a beanbag or a peace symbol that is passed around as people talk. It can also be a talk-it-out stick, which all people involved in the dispute hold onto with both hands, alternating hands. Each person lets go with one hand each time he or she speaks. If they get to the point where there are no hands on the stick and they still have more to say, they repeat as needed.

Practicing peace is not just for conflict; it also means learning everyday patterns of peaceable behavior. If they learn how to work on projects together, they may avoid some conflicts that erupt because of hurt feelings or people being excluded. With older children, allow them to suggest ways to show respect while working together. Fill in any areas they do not think of from these guidelines:

- Everyone gets a chance to say something.
- No putdowns are allowed. We will not judge any ideas as good or bad.
- After everyone has suggested ideas, we will say what works about each idea.
- When we make a presentation or poster, we will include everyone in the effort.
- We will decide in advance who will explain the group's work to the class. We will rehearse the explanation once to make sure everyone is satisfied.

If the children have ownership in the guidelines, it may help hold them accountable.

Prepare for Problem Solving

Before the children have any altercations, teach positive endings to interactions: thanking others for working with you, forgiving others, affirming good efforts in others. You can even develop a class prayer like this one to use in closing a conflict-resolution session:

O God, who is love, help us to turn away from our fights and to put away hard words and anger. O God, who forgives us, help us forgive others. May we remember that you made each one here and that you love us all. Thank you for being with us today. Help us live in peace. Amen.

Practice Problem Solving

Problem solving is used when there is conflict, or even to avert conflict when differences arise in a group. The process for problem solving is simple.

- Define the problem.
- Name all possible responses.
- Describe the consequences of responses.
- Choose a solution.
- Agree to try the process again if the solution does not work.

For example, suppose that some children routinely tease others at play time, and reactions are hostile. Help individuals choose appropriate behavior by practicing some problem solving as a group. You begin by having the children define the problem. Review any class rules about teasing. Then say, "We also need to know how to respond when someone teases us." Ask the group to name ways a child might respond when another child teases him or her. Possible responses include these:

- Call the child a name in return.
- Say something back.
- Tell a teacher.
- Ignore it.
- Wait until everyone is gone and then tell the teacher.
- Hit the other person.
- Get friends to gang up against the other child (form alliances in a kind of war).
- Throw something, such as a stick, at the person.

Accept all ideas without judgment, even if they are not reactions you would like to see. Honesty is important. If they do not suggest peaceful solutions, ask, "What are other ways you could respond? Are there ways that won't hurt anyone?" As you conclude, it is okay for you to add a few solutions, such as the following:

- Tell someone how you feel.
- Ask an adult for advice.
- Talk to a friend.

After you have a comprehensive list of responses, discuss possible outcomes from the various responses. Ask, "What would happen if you hit the person who teased you? What about if you told that person that your feelings were hurt?" Go through the list in a matter-of-fact manner, without labeling some choices as better than others. If children do not realize the danger of a response, it is your job to add such things as, "And I think if people started throwing sticks, someone's eye might get hurt. I will put that on our list."

Next, ask the children which responses a peacemaker might choose. Mark those. Ask each child to think about what the best solution for him or her would be. Find out what solution each person would choose. Point out the variety of workable solutions chosen within the group. It is important for children to realize that they are not locked into a particular response to a problem. They always have alternatives.

Roleplay Situations

Another way to practice peacemaking is by using roleplay. In a roleplay, you do not provide scripts. Roleplay will work best for children who are at least ten years of age or older. In roleplay, the children put themselves in the part and speak as if it were happening to them. For instance, if two children want the same computer game, different pairs of children might act out possibilities, such as taking turns, using a timer, the winner getting to keep playing, and so forth. The roleplaying exercise might develop like this:

Teacher: You two have been fighting over the game. I know you can work this out where both of you are satisfied.
First child: Okay, make it where the winner keeps playing.
Second child: No, you're so good that I won't ever get to play.
First child: Then, I'll play three games and then you can play.
Second child: That will take too long. Take turns after one game.
First child: Let's play together, then, but I have the controls; then you do next time.
Second child: Okay.
Teacher: Let's check. Any more solutions?
Second child: I think this one's okay. Let's do it.
Teacher: Let's check consequences, though. What is good and bad about the winner keeping on playing? about taking turns? about playing together? (*Children respond.*) Which works best for everyone?
Children: Playing together.
Teacher: Okay. It sounds like a solution that works for everyone. You'll both be at the game station, but you'll take turns working the controls, right?
Children: Right!

Of course, your roleplay might develop differently, since there is no script. People do not always come to an agreement so soon, either. If no solution is agreeable to both, start again.

When you take time to practice problem solving, after a while you will find children using it in their own conversations. If you also model problem solving in your own interactions with the children, they will learn the process faster.

Conflict Resolution

When people are together, there will be disagreements and problems. At least you have laid the groundwork for the steps toward peace. Here is what you could do when a fight occurs.

Part I

- First of all, be calm.
- Remind them that they know how to use the problem-solving process. This is what all your practice was for.
- Before you begin, always have children cool down first. Make sure they do not confuse cooldown with time-out. Cooldown is not a punishment. You are teaching them to put anger away before they try to work things out.
- When they are ready to negotiate, have them go to the peace corner or to the talk-it-out chairs you set up. Get out your talking stick or other item to be passed. Using a concrete object helps children know that they will have a turn to speak as many times as they need. (Make your own seat equidistant from both parties. If you sit next to one child, it may look as though you are taking sides.)
- Next, the children alternate turns talking. Each child gets several turns to say what happened. When he or she has spoken, the child passes on the talk-it-out item. The teacher's main role is to make sure there is no blaming, all the information has been discussed, and no one hurts another person. When you think everyone has described his or her experience, ask each person to sum up the other person's viewpoint. If they were not listening well enough to do so, begin the process again.

Once the positions are clear, help the process move on, or children may move forward on their own. The next step is when the children take turns naming a solution to the problem. (This is where your brainstorming practice comes in handy.) Have them talk about the consequences to each solution. Find out what solutions each child favors. Is there one they can agree on? If not, have them go back to suggesting solutions. Continue until a solution is found.

Part 2

To sum up, the final part of the process is
- Name solutions.
- Talk about consequences of solutions.
- Choose solutions agreeable to both parties.
- Pick the best one.

Have each person end with a positive response: thanking, forgiving, or affirming the other person. Sometimes the last negative feelings are dispelled if one person leads the way: "Thanks for working things out" or, "I appreciate that you kept at it." Younger children might say, "I am your friend" or, "Thank you." Prayer is sometimes an appropriate way to bring closure to this step.

Before the children leave the peace corner, have them agree to come back if the solution does not work. Check with them later to make sure they are working on their plan.

Part 3

- End positively.
- Agree to try again if needed.

Overcoming Barriers to Problem Solving

First John 3:18 encourages us to "love, not in word or speech, but in truth and action." First John continues with, "Those who say, 'I love God,' and hate their brothers or sisters, are liars; for those who do not love a brother or sister whom they have seen, cannot love God whom they have not seen. The commandment we have from him is this: those who love God must love their brothers and sisters also" (4:20-21).

Second Corinthians 5:18 tells us that we have been given the "ministry of reconciliation." We are called to put our faith into action, loving and reconciling with our brothers and sisters. As teachers, we must show children the way to do that, even when we meet obstacles. We have to find ways to overcome the barriers.

A common obstacle to peacemaking is the attention that a fight or conflict resolution attracts from other children. You have several options. First, do not try to address the problem within earshot of others. If the negotiators have observers, it is less likely that they will accept or suggest solutions that might make them lose face. Their classmates will be too prone to insert their opinions as well. If needed, find some extra help so that you can ensure privacy.

- See if another teacher can include your children in an activity while you work on peacemaking.
- Get the Sunday school superintendent to come in for a few moments.
- Ask a helper to show a video or to take the class on a listening trip out of the classroom.
- You might also ask the people involved in conflict to stay a few moments after you dismiss the others.

Another barrier to problem solving is when the children's viewpoints cannot be reconciled. They believe such different things about what happened that it is hard to name solutions because the problem cannot be defined. One technique a public school teacher used was to have each class member privately write down what he or she observed. Even if Sean insists that he never shoved anyone, you can be fairly sure what happened when fifteen out of sixteen children write, "I saw Sean push Jeremy into the fountain, and then Jeremy punched him." If you have rules about hitting or shoving others, impose the consequences of breaking the rules. Help the two children work out a plan so that the incident does not happen again.

If you have two children who can never get along, you may want to work with them on some project. And I mean work with them. Help them get started, and work right along beside them to supervise. You may be able to help them find a connection with each other. Some appropriate projects include these:

- Sponsoring a party for developmentally disabled adults
- Fixing furniture at a shelter
- Putting together mailings for the church office
- Refreshing bulletin boards
- Setting up a room for a meeting
- Cleaning out cabinets, pew pockets, or garden areas

Strength Circles

Some people find the problem-solving process itself to be a barrier because it focuses on problems first. An alternative is to have a strength circle. When there is a problem to resolve, the people involved sit in a circle. The facilitator lights a candle to symbolize God's presence. The facilitator poses a question and then passes an item (usually a cross, Bible, or other faith symbol) around the circle. Each person responds to the questions within a preset length of time. No one interrupts.

If there has been trouble with fighting in the afterschool room, for instance, the group would be invited to the circle, and the facilitator might pose the questions below, one at a time. The facilitator may answer first or last, but as with everyone else, may only state his or her own feelings, without blaming.

- What feelings have we just observed in our classroom?
- Are there things, such as not enough toys or not enough time to play, that caused fighting? Describe any.
- When there has been peace in the class, what helped make peace happen?
- What Bible stories might help us understand what we should do?
- For what do you need to be forgiven in this case, and what would you be willing to forgive?
- What is something good that could come out of this situation?
- How can there be peace in our group?
- What will you do next time?
- What action needs to be taken because the peace was broken?

After all comments, the facilitator summarizes comments and states the consensus about what needs to be done. If you, as the teacher, are the facilitator, proceed with the recommended action after the circle time. If someone else facilitates, they relay the consensus to you.

Strength circles rely on God's presence to help move the group to figure out next steps on a path of faithful living. It is a way to do conflict transformation rather than human problem solving. It is also more abstract and perhaps less suited for children. You might want to experiment with circles in the following ways.

Have a class come together to name ways they have been affected by time together. Questions might include these:

- What is a good memory you have from our class times together?
- What is something you learned?
- What will you want to learn more about next year?
- How have you grown closer to God during our time together?
- What do you think of when you first think of our class?
- How could we make the class better for next year's students?

Do something similar as children enter summer childcare. Ask these questions:

- What was your first reaction when you heard you were coming?
- What do you hope to enjoy while you are here?
- How will you expect to find God here?
- What can we do for you?
- What can you do for the group?
- How can this group serve God?

These circles are not conflict-transformation circles, but they will give you a feel for whether or not your group is able to try the concept.

Try It Out

Below are a variety of activities to help children practice peace. Some are written puzzles. Others help the children learn friendship skills, practice problem solving, or develop community.

Word Scramble (grades 3 through 6)

Materials: copies of the puzzle, pencils

Directions: Create a word puzzle using the following ideas. For younger children, you may need to leave the words unscrambled and let them match them to the correct place. For your convenience, the words are listed in the order they come in the puzzle, and the unscrambled answer is provided. When you actually make the puzzle, mix up the order of the words.

__ __ __ __ __ __ yourself.

Be __ __ __ __ __ __ __ __ __ of yourself and others.

Celebrate __ __ __ __ __ __ __ __ __ __ __ between you and others. Isn't it great that God has __ __ __ __ __ __ __ each of us unique?

Rejoice, __ __ __ __ always, and be __ __ __ __ __ __ __ __ __.

As God has loved us, __ __ __ __ one another.

Give your __ __ __ __ __ to God, for he __ __ __ __ __ for you.

Practice patience and __ __ __ __ __ __ __ __.

When you're sad, sing __ __ __ __ __ __ __ to God.

Remember, God loves you __ __ __ __ __ __.

Words to unscramble (going across) and fit above:

tapcec (accept)	groifnigv (forgiving)	freendiscef (differences)
tradeec (created)	ayrp (pray)	atflhnuk (thankful)
veol (love)	srace (cares)	ecsra(cares)
skidenns (kindness)	sairpes (praises)	lawsay (always)

Matching Puzzle (grades 4 through 6)

Materials: 3-by-5 cards with a definition or a word on each card

Directions: Have the students work in small groups to match the word with its correct definition.

- *Shalom*—A Hebrew word meaning peace, as well as wholeness and harmony
- *Harmony*—Lack of conflict or people getting along
- *Mediator*—Someone who helps people come to an agreement
- *Problem Solving*—A method for people to come to an agreement; involves listening, naming and discussing possible solutions, then choosing one
- *Pax*—Latin word for peace
- *Goodwill*—An attitude of wanting good things for others; sometimes called friendliness
- *Dispute*—A disagreement or conflict
- *Resolution*—An answer or end to conflict
- *Unity*—Oneness
- *Cooperate*—Work together
- *Compromise*—To come to an agreement by each person giving a little

Friend Flag (grades 2 through 6)

Materials: drawing paper, crayons or felt-tip markers

Directions: The following directions can be given verbally or can be posted in a learning center: Draw a rectangular flag. In a square on the left side of the flag, write words that describe a good friend. In a large shape at the bottom of the flag, write the names of people who are good friends. In another shape on the flag, write ways you have been a good friend. In another shape, write something new you could do to be a good friend.

Friendly Wheel (kindergarten through grade 6)

Materials: cardboard, brads, felt-tip marker, tape, scissors

Directions: Use felt-tip markers to divide a cardboard circle into sixteen sections. Write in the phrases below, one to a section. Cut out a spinner shape, and tape the spinner to a brad. Attach the brad to the center of the circle.

- Help someone carry something.
- Let someone else go first.
- Share with someone.
- Compliment someone.
- Listen to someone.

- Get someone a drink or a needed supply.
- Ask if you can help someone.
- Sit by someone you don't know.
- Sit by someone new to the group.
- Invite a new person to join you in a game or activity.
- Speak up for someone.
- Forgive someone.
- Get someone to tell about a hobby.
- Smile at other people.
- Say good things about three people.
- You decide what is friendly.

To Play: Children turn the spinner to let it choose for them a friendly act they will perform during the class or during the next week.

Talk About It (grades 3 through 6)

Directions: Discuss these situations:

Situation 1

Rachel: Were you at the party yesterday?

Sandra: Yeah, why?

Rachel: Melanie was her usual self.

Sandra: What do you mean?

Rachel: Acting like an idiot. I was so embarrassed to be at her table. I mean, I wish she would go away. How about you?

Remind the children that peacemakers need to learn to accept others. Ask, "How would Melanie feel if she heard them? How could Sandra respond out of respect for Melanie? How do you think Sandra feels?"

Situation 2

Josh: All right! We're tied. If we can just get Sam up to bat, we have a chance to win this one. Your turn at bat, Matt.

Matt: (*to self*) This is it. I've got to get on base. I can't strike out. (*Strike 1. Strike 2.*)

Josh: Matt, don't hold the bat like a nerd.

Matt: Here it comes. Here it comes. Oh, no! (*Misses the ball.*) I'm afraid to turn around. What is Josh going to say?

Ask, "What do you think Josh says? How does Matt feel? How does Josh feel? How can they demonstrate friendship?"

Play Human Bingo (kindergarten through grade 6)

Materials: pencils, bingo grid with characteristics written in each square (takes piano lessons, plays football, has a dog, and so forth)

Directions: To help the children understand some things they have in common, play human bingo. Give each child a bingo grid. Players sign one another's cards beside phrases that describe them. Limit the number of times any one person can sign another's card. For nonreaders, use pictures instead of words.

Problem Box (grades 3 through 6)

Materials: two shoe-sized boxes labeled "Response Box" and "Problem Box," pencils, blank index cards, index cards with one of the following statements written on each card

- Ask advice.
- Tell them you want to make peace.
- Walk away.
- Ignore it.
- Tell them how you feel.
- Talk to your parents.
- You have a choice. Ask yourself what else you could do.
- Pray.
- Don't allow others to be mean or hurtful.
- Try to understand why the other person is acting that way.
- Tell someone about it.
- Tell a teacher or adult who can do something.

Directions: Place the cards with the prepared statements in the Response Box. Hand out one or two blank index cards per person. Have each person write down a problem that needs solving. It can be a personal problem or a problem they have observed at school or in their neighborhood. Tell them not to sign the cards and to put them in the Problem Box.

When everyone has finished, draw one card at a time from the Problem Box and have someone draw a response card. (Once a response has been used, keep it out until all responses have been used. If you run out of responses, put them all back in.) Read the problem to the group, and have the other person read the selected response.

The group decides whether the response would be helpful. If not, they can suggest other responses. If you think of other responses that should be added to the Response Box, write them on blank cards and put them in the box.

You may want to practice first with the following problems:

- Everyone in my family treats me like I'm a baby.
- At Kids' Club, one kid does something mean for no reason.
- An older kid shouts nasty things at us when grownups are not around. We are all afraid of him, but the grownups don't believe us.
- This girl gets on my nerves by talking too much and complaining.
- Dad doesn't want me to hang around with my older cousin, but he's fun to be with.
- A girl at my school never obeys the teacher.
- Aides won't let me play a game at recess because I'm a girl.
- My sister always wants to play with me when I have friends over, and my mom says I have to let her.

Chapter Eleven

Helping Children Find Peace Within Themselves

This book began with your sense of peace and your spiritual practice of peace. You can lead children in countless activities that promote peace and set up an environment for conflict resolution; but with children, just as with adults, peace really begins inside. Conflict resolution may solve only specific problems, without addressing the causes of conflict or long-term patterns of behavior. To effect change, you also need to help the children find a sense of peace within.

Children may sing about the peace that passes understanding and is down in their heart, but do they really have peace inside? They can, with your guidance. Help them to have peace in their hearts by teaching them some spiritual disciplines.

Children are always looking to youth and adults as they learn how to live out the faith. Remember how we started our peace process by looking at our own spiritual practices. Start teaching your class about inner peace by describing your own habits of centering and prayer. Demonstrate and include prayer and meditation in class time. Encourage them to continue the practices at home.

Use Visuals

When you see children in constant motion, you may doubt that you can create a peaceful center for them during class. You can. First, incorporate prayerful moments into the flow of activities. Since the children need tangible examples, make it visual. Use pictures of outdoor scenes, and ask elementary children to spend three or four silent minutes looking at them and thinking about what the pictures could say about God.

In a similar way, ask them to look at pictures to find signs of God's love. Use nature pictures from travel magazines or Sunday school leaflets. These pictures might be natural vistas (cliffs, streams, or sunsets) or Christian symbols (doves or the Communion bread and chalice). Give each child a picture, with the picture side facing down. Tell the children not to turn their picture over. When you say, "Start," they turn it over and look at it. Give them three or four minutes of silence, or quietly play a recording of hymns to mark how long to reflect. When time is up, have the children form triads to tell about what they saw in the picture.

You can use the same approach to focus on concerns for prayer. Use pictures of people reconciling, praying, singing, hugging, playing, and so forth. Allow time afterward for each person to tell a neighbor what he or she thought about. Pray for the things they identified.

Collect all kinds of pictures of Jesus: healing, teaching, being with friends, sitting at the Last Supper, and so forth. Let the children pick their favorite one or two and think about what they like about it. Let them tell their neighbor why they chose the picture.

Use Artistic Expression in Prayer

Encourage the children to use art to express their thoughts. Pass out paper and crayons, and play quiet music. Ask them to draw a prayer to God. They can draw a prayer of thanksgiving or of a situation for which they need God's help. Tell them to try to draw without planning ahead, to let the crayon become the medium for the prayer.

Another hands-on spiritual exercise involves pipe cleaners or modeling dough. Ask older children to think quietly and to shape their medium into something that reminds them of God (or of family or of the class time together).

Prayerful art works better if you prepare children before the quiet time. Before art time, read to elementary children parts of 1 Corinthians 13, for instance. Ask them to think about God's love as they draw or paint.

Use Symbols

As symbols are used in worship, children will gather information over time by inference. They experience the symbolism and ritual before they fully understand it. A certain amount of mystery is involved in faith for both children and adults. Although children do not fully understand the abstract meaning of symbols, incorporate symbols into your class time to increase a sense of God's presence.

Light is a powerful symbol for both God's presence and our responsibility to live for Christ. Light one candle to be a Christ candle; then read John 8:12: "Again Jesus spoke to them, saying, 'I am the light of the world. Whoever follows me will never walk in darkness but will have the light of life.'" Turn off the lights and note the brilliance of the candle. Next, read Matthew 5:14, 16: "You are the light of the world.... Let your light shine before others, so that they may see your good works and give glory to your Father in heaven." Have the children come forward one at a time to light a candle from the Christ candle. Marvel at the gift of fire. Wonder how our lives can be lights to others. Note how much brighter the room is with all the candles burning. Pray that our actions will be like Jesus' example so that others will see Jesus' light in us. (Be careful. Use candles made for candlelight services, which have a sleeve to protect users from wax. Or keep the candles on a table and help each child light one with a lighter.)

Other symbols can be incorporated according to the lesson's focus. Place flat glass beads or small shells in a bowl of water. Have the children take a wet bead or shell from the water and carry it home to remember Jesus' baptism or their own. Make the whole classroom purple for Lent. Trace a cross on the children's foreheads with anointing oil and tell them that you are sending them out to continue holy habits.

Everyday Ideas

Wonder is akin to reflection. Take a few quiet moments to wonder and ponder. In the midst of any lesson, you can pose "I wonder" questions: "I wonder how Jesus felt when he started toward Jerusalem." "I wonder what the disciples' families were like?" "I wonder" questions do not have to have answers. Let the children wonder, too.

Keep more formal guided prayers short. For example, if you are studying Elijah, say something such as, "Close your eyes. In your imagination picture what I am saying. Think about when God came to Elijah. The wind blew in strong, noisy gusts. The earth shook. There was a great fire. But God was not in the mighty wind. God was not in the powerful earthquake or in the blazing fire. It was loud and wild, and then it got quiet. Quieter. Quiet. (*whisper*) And then Elijah heard God speak in a whisper. (*speak softly*) If God was going to whisper to you, what would

God say? Think about it a minute with your eyes closed. When I say to open your eyes, we will open our eyes and whisper our answers. What would God whisper to you?" (based on 1 Kings 19:11-13).

During guided prayer, it sometimes helps to relax. Encourage the children to get comfortable. Say, "Breathe in, and then breathe out slowly. Keep breathing slowly. Relax your muscles, first in your toes and feet, then in your legs and thighs, and then in your stomach and chest. Relax your arms and hands, and then your shoulders and neck and head." Ask the children to continue relaxing as they take deep breaths and think of God being next to them in the classroom. After a few moments, say, "Ask for God to be with you. God will be with you wherever you go."

Is quiet impossible for even a moment? Guided prayer can be a simple matter of focusing on the reason for being together. At the beginning of each session, say, "Feel yourself breathing in and out. Make your breath a prayer to God. Breathe out all your worries. Breathe in God's love. Pray that God will be with us today."

Praying While Moving

Prayer is not always done while sitting still. The labyrinth is a classic form of prayer and meditation that must be practiced while moving. A labyrinth is a winding path to a center. While people are going in, they release worries, fears, resentments, and extraneous thoughts. In the center, they try to be present to God and hear God speak to them. Going out, they try to stay with God as they move into the world. This is a form of contemplative prayer.

Move and pray in a similar format with children. While you are walking together to a prayer spot, tell the children to pretend to throw away their worries and fears. When you arrive, pray a short time in silence or sing soft praise choruses such as "Kum Ba Yah," "Alleluia," or other similar songs from your hymnal. As you walk back to your classroom, sing a praise song.

You can also ask the children to look for signs of God's love as you go on a silent walk. Or move around the building together, murmuring individual prayers for each thing or group you pass. The children may touch the items as they pray.

Take an elementary class to a park. Carry a canvas bag full of Scriptures, some of which are marked in a Bible, others on a cross-stitch hanging, poster, greeting card, or leaflet from Sunday school. Prop one Scripture up where everyone can see it. Ask these questions:

- What is God saying?
- What does this Bible verse mean for your life?

Ask the children to spend three to five minutes listening to God's world around them. Allow a few minutes for them to tell what they heard. Move to a new location and meditate on another Scripture.

More Ideas

- Confine your silent field trip to the classroom, with the children looking for religious items you hid in advance.
- Ask for silence as everyone writes thoughts after a lesson or story.
- Take a listening trip around the church to find signs of people fulfilling their ministry.
- Take a trip outdoors to listen for signs of spring. Allow for some quiet prayer time on the walk. Later, talk about what the children saw, heard, and felt.
- Pray first, then ask the children to look at a candle or other symbol for one minute of quiet.

Make Prayer Tangible

Provide media on which children can write their prayers. Keep silence as older-elementary children write prayers on their traced handprints. Cut the handprints out. Link the prayers together on a bulletin board.

Write prayers on rocks, wooden boards, parchment, or bark. Place them around the building, and then have a silent prayer walk from stop to stop.

Help preschoolers make a reminder to pray. Trace each child's hands and help him or her cut them out. Glue them onto paper, with the fingertips touching. Say, "The praying hands remind us to take time to talk to God. We need to plan times to listen to what God has to say to us." On the hands, record the children's prayer concerns. Send the prayer hands home to remind the children to pray there.

Spend time in class praying for individuals the children know. Do not be surprised if their prayer concerns include pets. Record the names of people for whom you pray, and regularly review the prayer journal together.

Make a prayer rock for each child to take home. Wrap a small rock in fabric and tie it with a ribbon. Attach a note: "Put me under your pillow to remind you to pray at night; then place me on the floor so that you will feel me and pray at morning light."

Calming Music and Movements

Soothe and relax children with restful music. Try instrumental arrangements of hymns played on classical guitar or folk instruments. You can purchase nature sounds, chants, and other calming sounds or music.

Use songs and movements that fall to silence, such as pretending with preschoolers to be a squirrel, a seed, or a leaf drifting or settling to the ground to be still.

Have a special countdown to use whenever the children need to relax: "5—Take a deep breath. 4—Stretch. 3—Let the chair (or floor) hold you up. 2—Make the love sign to remember that God always loves you. 1—Take a deep breath."

Teaching Prayer

Make prayer a regular part of class, but fit the length and form to the children's age levels. For instance, with younger children, ask what they would like to thank God for or what they would like to ask God for. Give a hug or hold the child's hand while you say a prayer right then, "God, help Jimmy's mother get well." Or, "Thank you, God, for Sally's new puppy."

With infants and toddlers, hold hands and repeat a simple grace at snack, and say thank-you prayers at circle time. When the children are three to five years old, begin asking for their concerns to add to prayers. When children can write, keep a prayer box on the table to put prayer requests in. Older children might want to write their own prayer that they could pray each time they come in the door. Send home several graces and bedtime prayers to choose from.

Let the children write prayers and learn the parts of prayer. First Thessalonians 5:17 says, "Pray without ceasing." Show the children how to do so. For instance, teach the children to make a PACT with God. Say, "The letters *P-A-C-T* can help you remember how to pray:

"Close your fist. Open each of your four fingers and touch them as you pray as follows:

- "Point to and touch your pointer finger as you give Praises to God. Name God's wonderful nature; praise who God is. That's *P.*
- "Add your middle finger. This finger is *A* for Asking God for forgiveness for wrongdoings. Also ask for things you need.

- "The ring finger is *C* for Coming Close to God. Spend time just listening for what God might say to you and thinking about or looking around for ways God is nearby through nature, music, silence, or Bible reading. You might ask for help in knowing God better.
- "The pinkie finger is *T* for Thanksgiving. Thank God for needed rain or sunshine, safety, fun, blessings, and so forth."

Pray the Word

You can also use Scripture to teach older children about prayer. They can model after the Lord's Prayer or use the Psalms as a guide.

Read aloud Luke 11:2-13, where Jesus taught his disciples to pray. Also read Luke 22:39-46, the story of Jesus' prayer at the Mount of Olives. Say, "In Luke, we read of how Jesus told his disciples to keep praying for what they need. We also find that one time Jesus struggled in prayer. Prayer can be hard work."

Ask, "When is it hard for you to pray? to keep on praying?" Say, "Often, people wish that God would take away hard situations. God's will is always the greater good for us. We would be missing God's best blessings if we chose our will rather than God's. It takes hard prayer to go forward sometimes, but, like Jesus, we will be given strength."

Use the Psalms as prayers. Have the children look through the Psalms to find verses or complete passages that could be used in these situations:
- When you need forgiveness
- When you want to praise God
- When you need hope
- When you need strength
- When you are sick or in trouble
- To thank God
- When you feel alone.

Help them find some verses to make a Psalm personal by substituting their names for the words *I* or *we*. Also change the verbs and pronouns to match. An example is Psalm 56:1, 2b-3: "Be gracious to Joe, O God... O Most High, when Joe is afraid, Joe puts his trust in you."

Find Peace

Teach the children an acronym that will help them find inner peace.

P = Praise God and remember God's greatness.

E = Empty fears and problems into God's hands.

A = Ask God for help.

C = Calmly wait for God's direction.

E = Expect God to creatively answer your prayer.

Tell the children that when they are worried or scared, they can carry out their P-E-A-C-E formula to trust in God and feel more at peace.

Make Space for Prayer

Make a quiet space in your room. It should not be the same area as the time-out spot. With preschoolers, a box or a corner might serve as the quiet spot. Furnish pillows or a beanbag chair. Provide older children with some paper so that they can write prayers or poems. You might provide older children with candles to light for each prayer request (in holders on a table, with supervision). They can also place marbles in a jar, one for each prayer; then transfer them to another jar, thanking God when the prayer is answered.

God Is With Us

Remember, you are not alone as you teach the children to have peace in their hearts. The Holy Spirit is at work before we are. God will guide you as you let the Holy Spirit work through you. Peace—it is a fruit of the Spirit.

Try It Out

The following activities can be used to help children make prayer a regular part of their lives.

Prayer Hands (ages 3 through 8)

Materials: paper, crayons

Directions: Help the children trace both hands on a sheet of paper. Above one hand, write "Prayer for Me." Above the other hand, write "Prayer for Others."

Choose three or four of the following sentences to let them finish. Have them write the sentences and their responses on the "Prayer for

Me" hand. With younger children, ask for their response and then write it on the hand.
- God, I hope you will...
- I pray my family will...
- God, help me love...
- God, forgive me for...
- God, I hope I will...
- God, help me...

Then choose three or four of the following sentences to let them finish. Have them write the sentences and their responses on the "Prayer for Others" hand.
- God, I pray for the world...
- I wonder...
- I pray for my church...
- I pray for my city (or town)...
- I pray for people around the world...
- I pray for those who are sick...
- I pray for those who are sad...
- I thank you for...

Journal Prayers (older elementary)

Materials: Folders with pockets, pencils, Bibles, copies of pages with the following directions:

Journal Page 1
Read Psalm 23.
- I can take better care of myself by...
- When I'm stressed, I can relax by...
- God brings me peace when...
- I can find peace by...
- I will be at peace with...
- I was a peacemaker when...

Journal Page 2
Read Isaiah 40:28-31. Focus on your own feelings:
- When I feel sad, I...
- I love to...
- I feel brave when...
- I worry about...
- I am afraid...

- I feel important when...
- I get angry when...
- When I'm tired, God can help me...
- When I'm discouraged, God will...

Journal Page 3

Read Isaiah 43:1-4.
- How does it feel to be precious to God?
- What do you think is God's special name for you?
- My good points are...
- My greatest talent is...
- I see myself as...
- The best thing about me is...
- I like...
- People think I am...
- I like people to tell me...
- I am proud that...
- I like to get attention by...
- I have power to...
- I'm learning to...
- How does God want you to use your gifts and talents?

Directions: Give each child a folder and one of the journal worksheets you have prepared. Let the children work alone to complete the worksheet. Consider making journaling a regular part of your classroom time, not every class but regularly enough so that it becomes familiar to the children. Journaling activities can easily be used in learning centers.

Chapter Twelve

Developing Resilience

When children grow up with adversity, neglect, and violence, you may think peace is impossible for them. However, something in the human spirit enables some people who have suffered greatly to emerge strong and healthy, with their best qualities refined. In other cases, adversity causes permanent brokenness. The ability to weather crises and grow up strong despite stresses is called resilience. The human spirit can indeed grow toward peace, even in unlikely circumstances.

How does resilience develop? A person's resilience has to do, first, with relationships with caring people. Resilience develops as children identify people they can trust and are taught limits that keep them safe. Resilient people have found safe places and anchors, people who listen to and believe in them.

Children become resilient when

- They are named, appreciated, and supervised as they are given tools for life.
- They are able to find mentors to help them mature.
- They have connections with trustworthy adults. These connections may take the form of parents talking with them and expecting them to achieve. It may happen as children experience informal mentoring in groups and sports.

Second, resilience concerns attitudes. Resilient people have developed an ability to find purpose and meaning in life, even in sad or stressful situations. They feel they can achieve things and be responsible. They can respect others and themselves. They can find ways to cope with problems. They can laugh at themselves. They also keep on keeping on despite setbacks.

These attitudes create a sense of hope for the future. When a person realizes that circumstances do not determine character or potential, hope and resilience flourish. Resilience also tends to be found in those who give to and help others. People who believe that what they do matters are more likely to bounce back from adversity. Resilient people tend to have a spiritual grounding.

Third, we create abundance and resilience in our life through ritual, which comforts through familiarity and structure, creates group identity, and makes us feel as if we belong to something important. Ritual carries meaning that layers over time. As we observe rituals year after year, we add deeper meanings to original understandings. Rituals form a history that shapes us throughout life. In times of fear or stress, rituals provide a bridge between the past and an unknown future. Rituals are one tool that resilient people use to overcome fears and adversity. Rituals are vessels for values passed from one generation to the next.

God's Story, Our Story

When we see history as God's story, we can find hope and strength. We realize that we are participants in God's story and are claimed by God and connected to those who have gone before us, both heroes and common people who achieved uncommon goals. When we see ourselves as part of God's story, we are not as isolated from other people, so we are more resilient.

We also find hope. God, who created everything, who is a promise-keeping and saving God, who hears the cries of all people, loves us and will watch over us. In the words of Jeremiah 29:11, "For surely I know the plans I have for you, says the LORD, plans for your welfare and not for harm, to give you a future with hope." God plans good things for us. What hope we can have. Hope creates resiliency because, no matter what, it is worth keeping on.

As you help the children know God's story and see themselves in it, you foster resilience. Elementary school children can learn to make the Bible their story by living out its message in their lives. Stories, memory verses, and Scripture songs can begin to form a reservoir for future needs for comfort and guidance. If this sounds like a big job, relax. You have some help.

Resilience and the Holy Spirit

In Galatians 5:22-23, we find: "By contrast, the fruit of the Spirit is love, joy, peace, patience, kindness, generosity, faithfulness, gentleness, and self-control." The discipline of living in the Spirit produces fruit, whether we live in good or bad times.

Intriguing similarities exist between the qualities that accompany resilience and the work of the Holy Spirit in a person. An attitude of giving surely springs from love, kindness, generosity, and self-control. Joy results in laughter. Patience, faithfulness, and self-control produce the ability to bounce back after setbacks and to find purpose and meaning in life. In fact, our faithful obedience to God is what causes us to observe religious rituals that help us find meaning. We would not seek mentors if we did not have love, patience, and self-control. A sense of peace and gentleness help us identify the safe places for us, and patience and faithfulness help us understand that circumstances do not determine our character.

Resilience does seem to be enhanced by the fruit of the Spirit. If we seek to live a Spirit-filled life, the Holy Spirit brings forth fruit in us that leads to wellness (peace) and resilience.

This means that you can trust the Spirit to work for peace in each child. You are called, however, to work with the Spirit. You build on the Spirit's work as you tell about God's transformations in the lives of ordinary people. Allow time also for the children to tell how God is working in their lives. Sometimes God speaks in the voices of our own children.

Let There Be Peace

When asked to draw her dream of peace, fifth grader Janet drew two children with different colors of skin working together. Todd, a fourth grader, drew people picking up litter and taking care of God's world. Sarah, a fifth grader, drew a peace sign. Together, sixth graders Frieda and Marta drew two people holding hands and a rainbow over their heads: God's promise to us. These concrete examples illustrate acceptance of others, responsibility, and a recognition that we need God's help for peace.

With God's help, the peace journey happens, from the two-year-old who offers a toy to an upset classmate, to a child who dreams of people getting along, to an adult who makes a commitment to live for peace. Our God is a God of peace, and God is with us.

God is present in your classroom as you learn from children, and even when you see a child hurt or bouncing back. Thank God for the grace that prepares you for the children, stands beside you, and transforms your efforts. Christ's advent on earth was accompanied by the angels' promise of peace. Thankfully, our God is a God of peace, and side by side we can sow seeds of peace. What a marvelous opportunity you have, as a teacher, to be a part of what God is doing. We can have peace in the classroom and in our lives.

Chapter Thirteen

More Help

The following resources will help you with further peace study, classroom activities, and teaching.

Resources for Peace Education

Early Childhood Adventures in Peacemaking: A Conflict Resolution Guide for Early Childhood Educators, by William J. Kreidler and Sandy Tsubokawa Whittall (Cambridge: Educators for Social Responsibility and Work/FamilyDirections, 1999).

Kids Creating Circles of Peace, by Anne Marie Witchger Hansen and Susan Vogt (St. Louis: Institute for Peace and Justice, 2000). Institute for Peace and Justice, 4144 Lindell Blvd. #408, St. Louis, MO 63108. Phone: 314-533-4445. E-mail: ipj@ipj-ppj.org. Website: www.ipj-ppj.org.

Learning the Skills of Peacemaking: A K–6 Activity Guide on Resolving Conflict, Communicating, Cooperating, by Naomi Drew (Carson, CA: Jalmar Press, 1995).

PowerXPress—Peacemakers (Nashville: Abingdon Press, 2002).

Together, by George Ella Lyon (New York: Orchard Books, 1994).

Posters, Charts

Emotions. Childswork/Childsplay, 135 Dupont Street, PO Box 760, Plainview, New York 11803-0760. Phone: 800-262-1886. Website: www.childswork.com. E-mail general information: info@ Childswork.com, customer service: customer@Childswork.com, ordering: orders@Childswork.com.

Kids' Conscious Acts for Peace. Educators for Social Responsibility, 23 Garden St., Cambridge, MA 02138. Phone: 617-492-1764. Website: www.esrnational.org.

For Conversations About Emotions

Alexander, Who's Not (Do You Hear Me? I Mean It!) Going to Move, by Judith Viorst, illustrated by Robin Preiss Glasser (New York: Atheneum Books, 1995).

Boundless Grace (Sequel to *Amazing Grace*), by Mary Hoffman, illustrated by Caroline Binch (New York: Dial Books for Young Readers, 1995).

Make Someone Smile: And 40 More Ways to Be a Peaceful Person, by Judy Lalli (Minneapolis: Free Spirit Publishing, 1996).

Today I Feel Silly: And Other Moods That Make My Day, by Jamie Lee Curtis, illustrated by Laura Cornell (New York: HarperCollins, 1998).

For Conversations About Fighting

The Big Book for Peace, edited by Ann Durell and Marilyn Sachs (New York: Dutton Children's Books, 1990).

The Brother's Promise, by Frances Harber, illustrated by Thor Wickstrom (Morton Grove, IL: Albert Whitman and Company, 1998).

The Hating Book (Reprint Edition), by Charlotte Zolotow, illustrated by Ben Shecter (New York: HarperCollins Children's Books, 1989).

The Meanest Thing to Say (Little Bill Books for Beginning Readers), by Bill Cosby, illustrated by Varnette P. Honeywood (New York: Scholastic, 1997).

For Talking About Valuing Self and Respecting Differences

What If Zebras Lost Their Stripes? by John Reitano, illustrated by William Haines (New York: Paulist Press, 1998).

Why Do You Love Me? by Dr. Laura Schlessinger with Martha Lambert, illustrated by Daniel McFeeley (New York: HarperCollins, 1999).

Devotional Reading for Children

My Journal: A Place to Write About God and Me, by Janet Knight and Lynn Gilliam (Nashville: Upper Room, 1999).

Pockets. Magazine published eleven times a year by the Upper Room (www.upperroom.org).

About the Labyrinth

The Labyrinth Online—www.labyrinthonline.com.

The Labyrinth Society—www.labyrinthsociety.org.

Veriditas, The World-Wide Labyrinth Project—www.gracecathedral.org/labyrinth.

How People Learn

Childhood and Society, by Erik H. Erikson (New York: W.W. Norton & Company, 1993).

Emotional Intelligence: Why It Can Matter More Than IQ, by Daniel Goleman (New York: Bantam Books, 1995).

Frames of Mind: The Theory of Multiple Intelligences, by Howard Gardner (New York: Basic Books, 1993).

Intelligence Reframed: Multiple Intelligences for the 21st Century, by Howard Gardner (New York: Basic Books 1999).

The Psychology of the Child, by Jean Piaget and Bärbel Inhelder (New York: Basic Books, 1969).

Appendix

This book was written to help teachers make peacemaking an undergirding principle that shapes the classroom environment, regardless of what lessons are being taught. The activities suggested are not intended to be used as a peace unit but rather to be integrated into your regular planning to help create a peaceful classroom.

However, there may be occasions when you do want to do a study or a retreat that focuses on peacemaking. In the following pages, you will find suggestions for using the activities in this book in such a study.

Four-Session Study (grades 3 through 6)

Session One: Developing Inner Peace

1. Talk About Peace

   Read Isaiah 55:12. Ask, "What is peace?" Record the children's answers on a piece of newsprint. Discuss the following questions:
   - What does it feel like to be calm inside?
   - What is peace?
   - What are synonyms for peace?

2. Practice Three Ways to Relax

   Introduce the class to the relaxation and deep-breathing exercises described in "Everyday Ideas" (pages 105–6). Then ask everyone to turn to a neighbor and make him or her laugh.

Discuss the following questions:
- Did you feel relaxed when you laughed? when you relaxed your muscles? when you breathed deeply?
- What are other ways to relax?

3. Make "Wanted Posters"

   See the directions on page 21.

4. Play "Like Me"

   See the directions on page 24.

5. Do "Daydream About Peace"

   See the directions on page 86.

Session Two: Identifying Feelings

1. Do a "Word Scramble"

   See the directions on page 97.

2. Make a "Feelings Chart"

   See the directions on page 37.

3. Play the "Feelings Game"

   See the directions on page 67.

4. Make a "Feelings Badge"

   See the directions on page 66.

5. Explore Actions to Deal With Feelings of Anger

   Have the children form triads, and ask each group to make up a skit about something that makes a person angry. Give them five minutes to work; then have them take turns acting out their skits. After each skit, ask how the angry person could cool down and react peacefully.

6. Play the "Burdens Race"

   See the directions on page 65.

7. Read a Story

   Read a story about emotions from the suggested resources list (page 118). Identify the emotions the characters express.

Session Three: Celebrating Diversity

1. **Imagine How Others Feel**

   Hold up pictures from books or magazines that show a variety of expressions (conflict, embarrassment, anger, joy, and so forth). Ask the children to imagine how the person in each picture feels. Allow time for several responses after each picture.

2. **Talk About Situations**

   Develop some typical open-ended situations that children in your class deal with. See "Talk About It" (page 99) for examples. At the end of each situation, ask, "What do you think happens next?" Have the children tell how each character might feel about the projected ending.

3. **Make a "We All Matter to God" Montage**

   See the directions on page 47. Read aloud Acts 10:34-35. Discuss what this passage says about how God feels about human differences.

4. **Affirm One Another**

   Have the group list twenty affirmations (comments or compliments that describe positive things about people: kind, friendly, forgiving, cheerful, helpful, and so forth).

   Write each child's name on a slip of paper and put the slips in a container. Have each child draw out another child's name and write an affirmation for the child whose name he or she drew. Discuss how it feels to be affirmed.

5. **Play "People Concentration"**

   See the directions on page 25.

Session Four: Making Peace With Friends and Family

1. **Talk About Kind and Unkind Actions**

   Explain that a hero is someone we respect because of courageous actions or caring behavior. Ask the children to name heroes. Show pictures of heroes from magazines or newspapers. Talk about the things heroes do.

   Point out that being friendly is part of peacemaking. Ask for examples of times friends have gotten angry or would not make peace. Ask what things children can do to make peace with friends in the kinds of situations named.

2. Make a "Friend Flag" or Play "Friendly Wheel"

See the directions on pages 98–99.

3. Learn About Becoming Better Friends

Suggest these three rules for becoming a better friend: smile, speak, listen. Smile at a person and speak to him or her, saying, "Hello" and asking a question, such as "How are you?" or "How was your weekend?" Listen to your friends so that they will feel important and will know you care about them. To have a friend, be a friend.

Read aloud Luke 19:1-10; Luke 10:38-42; or Luke 10:30-37. Let the children act out the story. Discuss these questions:
• How did it feel to be welcomed as a friend? to welcome others?
• How was the Samaritan a friend? How did it feel to need help? to be helped? to be the helper?

4. Do the "Problem Box"

See the directions on pages 100-1.

5. Experience Forgiveness and Forgiving

Remind the children that sometimes they are angry or sad because someone has hurt them. Sometimes they are the ones who hurt someone else. Forgiveness is important when there is hurt. We can ask God to forgive us when we have done wrong, and we can ask others to forgive us when we have hurt them. When we are the ones who have been hurt, we can forgive others.

Have each person record his or her wrong-doings and sins on paper and then rip or crush the paper. Pass around a wastebasket so that they can throw away the paper. Point out that God forgives us when we ask, and we are to forgive others. Repeat the exercise, having each person write down a person they need to forgive. Have them rip or crush those pages and throw them away also.

Pray, "God, be with us this and every day, teach us peaceful, loving ways. By your example, help us live in peace and love. Amen."

Four-Session Study
(kindergarten through grade 2)

Session One: Developing Inner Peace

1. Draw Pictures of Peace

   Play quiet music, and ask the children to draw a peaceful picture. Encourage the children to tell you about their pictures.

2. Practice Three Ways to Relax

   Introduce the class to the relaxation and deep-breathing exercises described in "Everyday Ideas" (pages 105–6). Then ask everyone to turn to a neighbor and make him or her laugh.

   Discuss the following questions:
   • Did you feel relaxed when you laughed? when you relaxed your muscles? when you breathed deeply?
   • What are other ways to relax?

3. Make "Wanted Posters"

   See the directions on page 21.

4. Play "Like Me"

   See the directions on page 24.

5. Read a Story About Peace

   Choose one of the books listed on page 118.

Session Two: Identifying Feelings

1. Make Feelings Puppets

   Let each child decorate a paper plate to show a happy face on one side and a sad face on the other side. Tape a wide craft stick at the neck position to use as a handle.

   Describe a variety of situations; then let the children hold up the happy face or the sad face to show how they would feel. Remind the children that God is with them no matter how they feel.

   Read a suggested book about feelings (page 118) and have the children use their puppets to reflect the feelings expressed by characters in the story. Explain the conflict resolution guidelines described on page 37. Ask what conflict resolution technique could be used in the story.

2. Make a Mural

   Let the children tear pictures out of magazines that show various feelings. Have them paste the pictures on a large sheet of paper.

   Ask, "Who can touch a picture of someone who might be angry? Raise your hand." Let a person who raised his or her hand approach the pictures and touch one. Ask: "Who can touch a picture of someone who is excited?" Continue asking about feelings, using the words listed for the "Feelings Chart" (page 37). Next, ask the children to each touch a picture of a person who shows a feeling they have felt before.

3. Use the "Feelings Thermometer"

   See the directions on page 66.

4. Explore Actions to Deal With Feelings of Anger

   Have the children form triads, and ask each group to make up a skit about something that makes a person angry. Give them five minutes to work; then have them take turns acting out their skits. After each skit, ask how the angry person could cool down and react peacefully.

5. Play the "Burdens Race"

   See the directions on page 65.

Session Three: Celebrating Diversity

1. Imagine How Others Feel

   Hold up pictures from books or magazines that show a variety of expressions (conflict, embarrassment, anger, joy, and so forth). Ask the children to imagine how the person in each picture feels. Allow time for several responses after each picture.

2. Talk About Situations

   Develop some typical open-ended situations that children in your class deal with. See "Talk About It" (page 99) for examples. At the end of each situation, ask, "What do you think happens next?" Have the children tell how each character might feel about the projected ending.

3. Make a "We All Matter to God" Montage

   See the directions on page 47.

4. Affirm the Children

Have the group list twenty affirmations (comments or compliments that describe positive things about people: kind, friendly, forgiving, cheerful, helpful, and so forth).

Go around the class and use a positive comment to describe each child.

5. Play "People Concentration"

See the directions on page 25.

Session Four: Making Peace With Friends and Family

1. Play "Thumbs Up"

See the directions on page 67.

2. Play "Like Me"

See the directions on page 24.

3. Make a Forgiveness Mobile

Cut out a large heart from posterboard, punch a hole at the top, and string yarn through the hole. Help the children write on one side "I Forgive" and on the other "Forgive Me."

Talk about times when we need to be forgiven: when we call someone names, when we hurt someone, when we lie or cheat. Write some of the examples on the "Forgive Me" side. Have them name times when we forgive others for things such as pushing or taking things. Write those examples on the "I Forgive" side. Say, "God forgives us when we hurt others. God asks us to forgive others." Hang the mobile in the classroom.

4. Help Children See Themselves as Peacemakers

Say, "God has created each one of us unique. A peacemaker knows that he or she was created wonderfully by God. So, if you are a peacemaker, you know you are great. Who knows you are great? (*Have a show of hands.*) Great! We are peacemakers that way.

"A peacemaker also practices kindness with others and names what is good about other people. Who can name a good thing about a neighbor? (*Let the children respond or raise hands.*) A peacemaker tries not to hurt others. A peacemaker forgives when people are hurtful. Raise your hand if you have forgiven someone. A peacemaker tries to solve problems so that everyone wins. These are all things we can do."

Form a circle. Affirm each child. Shake hands or put a hand on an arm or a shoulder. Look into the child's eyes while you say something positive about him or her. Have everyone repeat after you, "Our God is a God of peace. We can make peace."